itty-bitty hats

itty-bitty hats

cute and cuddly caps to knit
for babies and toddlers

Susan B. Anderson

ARTISAN
NEW YORK

Published by Artisan

A Division of Workman Publishing, Inc.

708 Broadway

New York, New York 10003-9555

www.artisanbooks.com

Library of Congress Cataloging-in-Publication Data

Anderson, Susan B.

Itty-bitty hats : cute and cuddly caps to knit for babies and toddlers / Susan B. Anderson.

p. cm.

Includes bibliographical references.

ISBN 1-57965-295-6

1. Knitting—Patterns. 2. Caps (Headgear) 3. Infants' clothing. I. Title.

TT825.A54 2006

746.43'20432—dc22   2005055870

Printed in Malaysia

10 9 8 7 6 5 4 3 2 1

Book design by Jan Derevjanik

Brian, the love of my life and father extraordinaire,
our fantastic four—Evan, Ben, Holly, and Mary Kate—
and my hero, Mary Ann Barrett.

contents

introduction

I STARTED KNITTING AT AGE NINETEEN WITH AN INSTRUCTION booklet, acrylic yarn, and needles from a fabric store. Most important, I had the determination to learn on my own. At that time, about twenty years ago, knitting wasn't as popular as it is today. I knew absolutely no one who knitted, and certainly teenagers such as me weren't knitting. I struggled and struggled, but in my own funny way, I began a love affair with knitting that hasn't wavered over the last two decades. Being a self-taught knitter, I have always figured out my own solutions for creating finished products. Sometimes I have gone about things in an unusual way, but as a result, I feel as though I can create almost anything through knitting. If I make mistakes along the way, I don't worry about them too much. Instead, I try to find a new way to make things work. Upon completion of every finished project, I still get a feeling of exhilaration and satisfaction. This feeling of joy, curiosity, and excitement about knitting is what I want to share with you in this book.

About ten years ago, after knitting seemingly every conceivable project, I knit my first baby hat, and a new journey began. On completion of that red cotton hat, I felt a lightbulb come on in my head. Something about that hat just fit. First of all, I love babies. More specifically, I love babies' heads. What could be better? Delicious chubby cheeks, soft fuzzy hair, cuddly ears, the backs of their necks—I could drink them in forever.

The idea of focusing on baby hats came so naturally to me, it seems like fate. Having four young children of my own, I already had enough heads to cover for a lifetime. I started slowly creating and refining the perfect baby hat. I measured lengths from crown to ear; I tried as many different styles as I could imagine and maybe some I didn't. Every time I finished one hat, I ran straight back to my needles to start another one. I have never tired of creating hats, for one reason: Everyone loves a baby in a great knitted hat! This simple act of knitting a hat has brought more joy to people than I could ever have guessed. You will see the happiness it creates when you begin your own journey in hat making.

The patterns in this book are meant for every knitter, whether novice or experienced. When you begin knitting these hats, you'll see that the sky is the limit. Try everything. Add your own colors. Mix and match embellishments and styles. Create, create, create. Anyone can do it.

The many baby hat classes I have taught over the past couple of years have only inspired me more. I have taught grandmas, young and not-so-young mothers, expectant mothers, teenagers, aunts, friends—you name them, they learned to make wonderful baby hats. After two short classes, everyone (yes, everyone!) went home with a completed baby hat. To their amazement, it is not as difficult as it appears, and for me, that is the thrill of it. It is like letting people in on a really fun secret. The accomplishment these students felt is gratifying beyond words.

If you have made a scarf (or twenty), it is time to move on. Hats are the perfect next step. Start with a simple, one-color hat to hone your techniques. I guarantee that you will want to add an embellishment, stripe, ribbon, or appliqué to your next hat—maybe even to the one you have just made.

My knitting philosophy embodies an easy, fun style that keeps things simple. When knitting, I never like to be too tied to a pattern. That is why a lot of the embellishments on my hats are put on after the main knitting is completed. This makes it easier to simply enjoy the knitting process. Perspective is also important when I am designing. I like to think about the big people looking down at the baby or toddler and what they will see. Keeping this in mind, I love to make the hats fun to look at from above. When people see the baby you love wearing one of these hats, you will see them burst out in a smile or giggle. I hope new knitters realize they can start simply, then quickly add new dimensions of their own choosing to their knitting repertoire. I also hope experienced knitters will find new inspiration here. Knitting represents love at its finest, and who better to shower this love on than a baby?

Knit for beautiful babies everywhere. Enjoy!

what you need

I wish someone had given me direct guidance in selecting the materials I would work with throughout my knitting life. I would have saved a lot of money and time along the way. I'd like to offer that guidance to you. In this chapter, I'll describe the variety of tools you will need for knitting, and I'll also provide you insight into some of my specific favorites. I have done much research on tools—through trial and error—throughout the years. Please consider my recommendations, then choose what feels right and comfortable for you as you develop your own knitting style.

KNITTING NEEDLES

Combine needles with yarn and you don't need much else, which is why knitting is ultimately such a simple art. Using the correct needles for your projects is key to achieving delightful results. Needles come in many materials, lengths, and sizes. They also may be straight, circular, or double-pointed. You have a lot to choose from, and the more you knit, the more particular you will become about the needles you work with.

Different types of needles work better for different projects. For baby caps, I find that circular needles and double-pointed needles work best. Although circular needles are designed for knitting in the round, in order to form a seamless tube, I use them not only for knitting in the round but for knitting back and forth as well. In fact, I don't use straight needles at all. Learning to knit on circular needles is a benefit because you are immediately comfortable with using them. The advantages are many. You can put an enormous number of stitches on longer circular needles, and since the stitches rest on the cable, they are not as cumbersome to maneuver when you are knitting. You can knit in compact spaces with circular needles because your knitting is held directly in front of you or on your lap. This also creates less stress on your arms and hands. My favorite lengths for circular needles are 16 inches for hats and 24 inches for just about any other project.

For finishing a project like the top of a hat, you will need double-pointed needles. My preference is 7-inch needles made of wood. The pattern you are using will tell you how many you will need.

In general, beginners may prefer wood or bamboo straight needles because they aren't as slippery and are conducive to slower knitting. Faster knitters—or knitters who want to become faster—should use metal needles because of their smooth, slippery surface. The stitches move quickly, and you won't have to push and pull as you knit.

My current favorites are Skacel Addi Turbo circular needles and Lantern Moon ebony double-pointed needles in the 7-inch length.

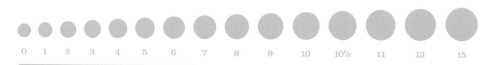

| 0 | 1 | 2 | 3 | 4 | 5 | 6 | 7 | 8 | 9 | 10 | 10½ | 11 | 13 | 15 |

NEEDLE GAUGE

To find the size of your needles, you can use a needle gauge, which looks like this. Simply put the point of the needle into a hole: The hole that exactly fits is the correct size.

PINS AND OTHER SUPPLIES

pins and stitch markers • I use coilless safety pins to mark the beginning of the round or other important areas in my knitting, in place of a stitch marker. I pin the safety pin directly onto the fabric, in between the first and last stitches of the round, to mark the beginning, and I move the pin up as I knit the base of the hat. Stitch markers are small rings placed on your needle or attached to the knitted fabric to mark your place. I stop and start a lot when I'm knitting, so this has always been easier for me. Safety pins can also be used to hold a small number of stitches as a stitch holder would (see page 14) or to pin on embellishments while finishing.

straight pins • You'll use straight pins for securing embellishments before sewing them on, and for pinning seams when finishing garments.

yarn needle • Yarn needles or tapestry needles are fat sewing needles with a large eye for threading yarn through. They are used for sewing seams, sewing on embellishments, weaving in ends, embroidering, and more. These needles are a must-have for knitting. My current favorites are Goldtone bent-tip yarn needles.

FAVORITE LUXURIES

The **Pom Tree** is the best tool available for making tassels, pom-poms, and fringe and for cutting lengths of yarn or ribbons. It is far simpler than the other types of pom-pom tools, particularly those that require winding yarn around a circle.

The Jordana Paige Knitter's Purse, in black, is my all-time favorite **knitting bag**. The shape is sleek and stylish, the pockets are perfect, and the upright standing form is excellent.

IMPORTANT EXTRAS

Good-quality, sharp **scissors** are essential when knitting. My current favorites are Fiskars scissors for home. A small 7-inch **ruler** or **tape measure** is necessary to measure the length of your knitting. A **notepad, Post-it Notes**, and a **pencil** are helpful to keep track of where you are in your pattern or give you a place to jot down a great idea. Knitting is all about numbers of stitches, so you will be surprised how often you will need a **calculator** to figure out one thing or another in your patterns. **Stitch holders**, which look like large safety pins, are used to hold stitches that aren't bound off but need to be set aside and worked on later. Double-ended stitch holders are a particularly nice option. A **cable needle** is used to hold stitches when knitting cables (see page 33), although a double-pointed needle can be used in place of a cable needle at times. **Crochet hooks** are wonderful for picking up a dropped stitch, creating an edging or embellishment, and weaving in ends.

YARN

The vast variety of available yarn can seem endless and overwhelming at times. However, the choice is simplified when making baby hats. I recommend using the yarns suggested in the patterns because I felt they were the best choices for the purpose and appearance of each hat. These yarns are mainly made of cotton and wool, with some blends, and they range in weight from DK (double-knitting, also known as sport) to light worsted weight, worsted weight, and heavy worsted weight. You will get between 4 and 5 stitches per inch using these yarns. The weight of the yarn determines the size needles you will use and how the finished knitted product will look. I purposely used the same yarns and the same weights of yarn in many of the patterns so you can knit many hats with the yarn you purchase. You can substitute different yarn for the patterns, but then be thorough about checking the gauge and finding a yarn with similar qualities (see page 17).

Many yarn shops will wind yarn for you when you purchase it at the shop. Other options for hand-winding yarn include using your friend's or child's hands (then you get to visit while winding) or the back of a chair to hold the skein open. This works just as well as fancy equipment. Winding yarn by hand can help you get a feel for the yarn and can be relaxing, too.

Winding a ball of yarn is fun, and everyone has his or her own style. Always try to wind your ball a little loosely so the yarn doesn't become stretched. Begin by taking the loose end of the skein and winding it around your left pointer finger and middle finger several times. Slide this little ball from your fingers and begin winding the yarn around it. Wind five to ten wraps in one direction, then turn the ball in a different direction and continue wrapping the yarn. Keep turning the ball while winding to keep the yarn evenly distributed and to ensure a round shape at the end.

TIPS ABOUT YARN

- Make sure you wind yarn that comes in skeins twisted together in a figure-eight fashion. If you try to knit without winding the skein of yarn, you will have a tangled mess that will take many hours to straighten out.

- For any of the hats in this book that use multiple colors, you don't have to use as many as suggested. If you don't want to buy seven different colors, try using two or three. You can achieve fantastic looks using only a few colors.

- Buy the best-quality yarn you can afford. It makes a difference, and it does show in your work. High quality doesn't always mean expensive.

- Always try to support your local yarn shops when buying yarn, but if you can't get out to a shop, which can be trying with little ones running around or if you aren't mobile, don't forget the wonderful catalog and Internet shopping available.

- Look through this book thoroughly before you begin. Select the patterns you most want to knit, but also see how the yarn called for can overlap with other projects in the book. When knitting small projects, you often end up with a lot of leftover yarn. I intentionally repeated the same yarns and gauges throughout the collection to maximize the number of projects your yarn selection can make. I use leftover yarn from past projects constantly, and you will, too, if you start using many colors at once.

sketch book

pom tree

circular needles

GAUGE

Gauge is the most important element of making a terrific-fitting garment. Gauge is the number of stitches you get in one inch of your knitting when using a certain weight of yarn and size of needles.

I had a student become very upset because the hat she was working on was way too big. She couldn't understand why. We measured her gauge and found she was knitting at 4½ stitches per inch, when the gauge for the pattern she was making required 5 stitches per inch. That may seem close enough, but she added an extra 2 inches to the circumference of her hat by not knitting to gauge! Checking gauge is one of the most important aspects of knitting. When you start paying attention to gauge, you will discover if you knit loosely, tightly, or right on the mark. Then you can adjust your needle size for your style of knitting. Hats should fit snugly on the head, so it is important to knit at the correct gauge for these patterns. Checking gauge is simpler than it seems, and it becomes second nature after a while.

When working with a new yarn or starting a new pattern, make a swatch as follows:

1. With your selected yarn and needles, cast on 20 stitches.

2. Knit in pattern stitch for 4 inches.

3. Slip the knitted fabric off the needle without casting off.

4. Lay the swatch flat on a table and let the yarn take its natural shape. Do not tug or stretch the fabric.

5. Set your ruler on top of the knitting with the right side of the fabric facing you.

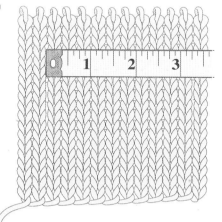

6. Choosing a section near the center of the swatch, count how many stitches there are in one inch.

> TIP • Many times, when a project is small, you can begin it as directed in the pattern, knowing that after you have knitted a couple of inches, you can check your gauge.

substituting yarns • Make sure the yarn you are substituting has the same gauge as is called for in the pattern. One easy way to tell if a different yarn might work is if the weight is conveyed in the name of the yarn. For example, RYC Cashcotton DK could be easily substituted for RYC Cashsoft DK (but make a gauge swatch first to be safe). DK (double-knitting) describes the weight and gauge of this yarn. You can also read the label to get the recommended gauge of the yarn and compare it to the required gauge listed in the pattern.

KEY INFORMATION FOR GAUGE AND NEEDLE SIZE:

- If the number of the stitches in one inch of your swatch matches the required number of stitches per inch in the pattern, then you are ready to start.

- If there are too many stitches per inch, use larger needles.

- If there are too few stitches per inch, use smaller needles.

- If you need to change needle size, move up or down by one size. Keep making new swatches until you obtain the correct gauge.

TIP • You can keep a swatch library in a knitting journal. In it, record the yarn information, gauge, and the size needles used for each swatch. Then you have a handy resource about your own personal knitting. To save your swatch, bind off the stitches (see page 30) to remove the swatch from the needles.

let's knit

This instruction section covers the skills needed to knit the projects in this collection. I am sharing with you the skills and techniques I use and prefer. There are many ways to go about knitting, and if you prefer using a different technique to achieve the same finished product, then stick with what you are doing. There are no steadfast rules in knitting, and you need to feel comfortable and have fun while you are creating. With that being said, here are the knitting techniques I recommend.

basic stitches

CASTING ON

slip knot • The slip knot is the very first step in casting on to begin your project.

1. Measure out the length of yarn needed for the long-tail cast-on (which you'll learn below). The pattern you are about to begin will tell you how many stitches you will need to cast on. You can figure out how long the tail of the yarn needs to be by wrapping the yarn around the needle once for every stitch called for. Then add about another 8 inches. At this point on the yarn, you will make a slip knot.

2. Make a loop, overlapping the yarn at the bottom of the loop.

3. Bring the yarn that is on top of the overlap behind and then through the loop, making another loop. Pull up.

4. Put the new loop on the needle and tighten it to fit.

   TIP • Always include the slip knot when counting stitches!

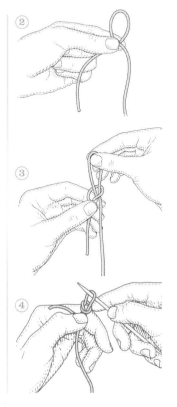

long-tail cast-on • I use this method of casting on for almost every project I start. I think it looks clean, and it gives the right amount of stretch to my work.

1. With the slip knot on the needle, hold the needle with your right hand and let the yarn hang down. The yarn attached to the ball (the working yarn) should be behind the needle, and the yarn tail should be toward you.

2. Pinch the index finger and thumb of your left hand together and stick them between the strands of yarn hanging from the needle.

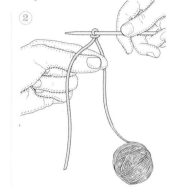

3. Open up your left index finger and thumb. The tail end of the yarn will be over your left thumb, and the working yarn will be over your index finger. Turn your hand so your palm is facing you, and hold both strands of yarn against your palm with the other fingers of your left hand.

4. Imagining your left thumb is your left needle, bring the right needle point around the outside of the yarn on your thumb, then under the yarn. Then bring your needle around the outside of and under the yarn on your index finger. Turn the needle downward and pull it back through the yarn around your thumb. Gently slip the yarn from around your thumb.

5. Without dropping the yarn held on your palm, put your thumb back under the tail end of the yarn and pull the stitch up tight on the needle.

• Repeat steps 4 and 5 until you have the required number of stitches on your needle. Remember to count your slip knot as one stitch.

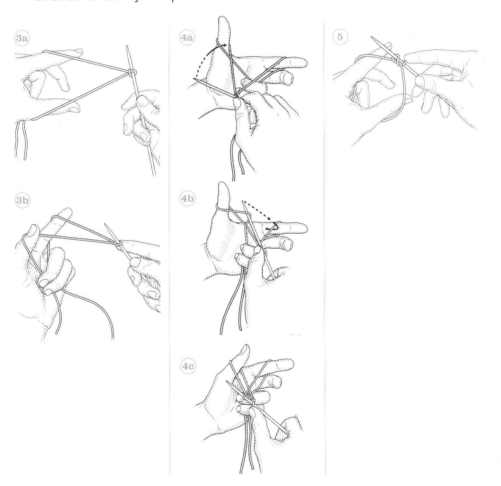

backward-loop or single cast-on • This type of cast-on is used for casting on in the middle of a row, for casting on at the end of a row, and for making a picot edging. It is simple and easy for children and anyone just learning to knit.

1. Make a slip knot with a short tail about 8 inches long, as you'll only use yarn attached to the ball for casting on with this method. Put the slip knot on the needle and tighten it. Hold the needle in your right hand.

2. Place the working yarn across your left palm (your palm is facing you) and gently put your fingers over the yarn. Wrap the yarn around the outside of your thumb.

3. Imagining your left thumb is your left needle, put the point of the right needle under and through the loop of yarn formed around your thumb.

4. Gently pull your thumb out of the loop and tighten the new stitch on your needle. Wrap the yarn around your thumb.

• Repeat steps 3 and 4 until the desired number of stitches are on your needle.

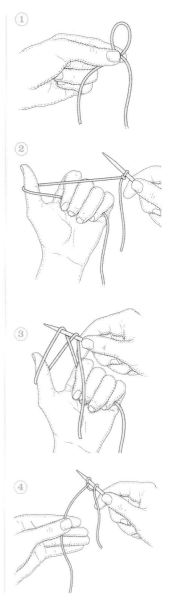

continental method • Really, only two stitches are used to create all knitted projects: the knit stitch and the purl stitch. Once beginners understand this, they realize how simple knitting can be. There are different styles or methods of knitting, which means people hold their hands and yarn in different ways. Amazingly, all of these methods produce the same results, which means it is okay to hold your hands in a way that is comfortable for you as long as you are getting a result you're happy with. I use the Continental method of knitting. I highly recommend you learn and use this method of knitting for speed, gauge accuracy, and comfort. However, use whatever method works for you and your body. Many new knitters struggle with the Continental method right away and need to "throw" or wrap the yarn with their right hand in order to understand the concepts (this technique is known as the English or American method). After they get comfortable, some of them change over to the Continental method.

When I was nineteen and working as a lifeguard, I was passing my off-duty time by knitting (I first began knitting by holding the yarn in my right hand and throwing). As I was sitting on a bench by the pool, a woman I didn't know walked up behind me, grabbed my arms and hands, and said, "You must knit like this!" She quickly and briskly moved my hands and the yarn, showing me the Continental method of knitting. This took all of about 10 seconds, and then she just walked away. I was taken aback and slightly insulted. I couldn't understand why she did this, but I *never* knitted by throwing the yarn again. I was scared into the Continental style. That was the only knitting instruction I ever received, and I wish I could thank her now, because it was the best thing for my knitting. But what a way to start!

knit stitch • The knit stitch is the basis for every project. Remember, as you knit, you are always taking stitches from the left needle and knitting them onto the right needle. After you knit the first stitch, the yarn will always be coming from your right needle. Also, always make sure you are knitting with the working yarn (the yarn attached to the ball) and not the tail. This is a common mistake.

TIP • If you are new and don't feel ready to dive right into the first project, make a slip knot, cast 12 stitches onto a pair of straight needles or 24-inch circular needles, and practice by knitting back and forth on these stitches.

When you knit back and forth, you will knit until all the stitches are on the right needle. Then you will turn your work around to work back in the other direction. When you turn your work around, put the needle holding the stitches into your left hand and begin transferring the stitches to the right needle again.

1. Hold the needle with the cast-on stitches in your left hand with the yarn over your left index finger.

   TIP • I squeeze the yarn between my index finger and middle finger at the knuckle in order to have tension, but others in addition wrap the yarn around their ring finger or little finger or find other ways to make the yarn taut. Experiment to discover what works best for you.

2. With your right hand, place the point of the right needle into the first loop on the left needle, inserting the needle point from bottom to top and from front to back (behind the left needle). The points of the needles will make an X. Hold the X together with your right hand, with your thumb in front and your index finger in back.

3. Wrap the yarn from the index finger counterclockwise around the point of the right needle. After wrapping, the yarn should end up at the back of the right needle. Tip the point of the right needle downward and pull the loop through the stitch, keeping the loop on the right needle.

4. Slip the completed stitch off the left needle. The new stitch is now on the right needle.

   • Here is a chant for you to say to yourself as you knit the four steps of the knit stitch:
   In (2),
   Around (3a),
   Out (3b),
   Off (4).

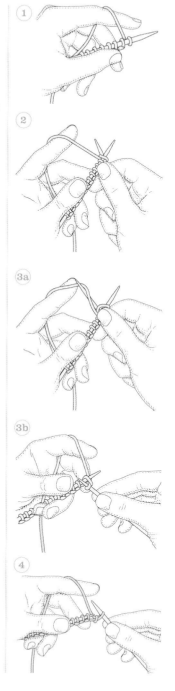

purl stitch • The second stitch in knitting is the purl stitch. The purl stitch is really just a knit stitch worked from the back. After you have the knit stitch down, the way to make different stitch patterns is to learn the purl stitch. You can make textures in your knitting by combining these two stitches. As with the knit stitch, you'll be taking the stitches from the left needle and slipping them onto the right needle.

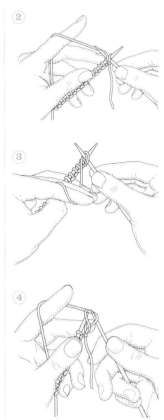

1. Hold the stitches on the left needle with the working yarn in front. Hold the yarn over your left index finger. The tension on the yarn is created by squeezing the yarn between the index and middle finger of your left hand.

2. Insert the right needle from right to left through the front of the first stitch. The points of the needles make an X.

3. With your left index finger, bring the yarn up and over and down behind the right needle. When you bring the yarn down, squeeze it between the index and middle finger of your left hand to keep the yarn taut.

4. Tip the point of the right needle upward and bring the loop back through the stitch and onto the right needle.

5. Slip the completed stitch off the left needle. The new purl stitch is now on the right needle.

identifying knit and purl stitches • You will need to able to know if you are on the knit side or the purl side of your knitting. If you are knitting back and forth on straight needles, you'll need to know whether to knit or purl the next row once you pick up your knitting after setting it down. You also need to identify individual stitches if knit and purl are being used on the same row to create a stitch pattern such as ribbing or seed stitch. Being able to identify the two types of stitches, knit and purl, helps you read your knitting and know what to do next.

knit stitches • When you are looking at the knit stitches, you will see a V shape to the stitches, and the fabric will be smooth. When the knit stitch is on the needle, the same holds true: You will see a V shape just below the loops on your needle.

purl stitches • When you are looking at the purl stitches, you will see a loop shape to the stitches, and the fabric will be bumpy. When the purl stitch is on the needle, there is one loop just below the needle.

KNITTING IN THE ROUND

knitting in the round on circular needles • Circular needles are two needles that are joined by a cable. They are used for both knitting in the round and knitting back and forth. The length of the needles, measured from tip to tip, is determined by the cable length. Most of the hats in this collection are knit in the round on a 16-inch set of needles. Even though the needles are attached, consider them separate needles, holding one needle in your right hand and the other in your left hand. The following steps will start you on your way.

1. Cast on just as you would if you were knitting back and forth.

2. After you have completed casting on, spread the stitches all the way around the needles and the cable so the first and last stitches come together at the points of the needles.

3. *Most important,* make sure the stitches are not twisted before you begin knitting. Look to see if the cast-on row is at the inside of the circle as you hold the needles up. If the stitches are twisted, then untwist them at this time. There is no way to untwist stitches once you've started knitting. The only way to fix this is to start over.

4. Place a stitch marker on the right needle before you begin knitting to mark the beginning of the round. Do this by sliding a stitch marker onto the point of your right needle.

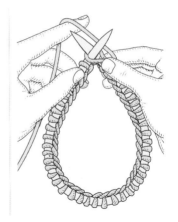

5. Hold the left needle in your left hand and the right needle in your right hand. Be sure the yarn is coming from the needle in your right hand.

6. Begin working in the round by knitting the first stitch on the left needle as you usually would (again, making sure the yarn is coming from your right needle). Now you have joined the circle.

7. Continue knitting as your pattern directs until you reach your desired length, slipping the stitch marker from the left to the right needle as you begin each new round. Slide the stitches along the cable as you knit.

- The easy part of knitting in the round is that you are knitting in a continuous circle, there is no turning back and forth, and there are no seams to sew at the end. Many people prefer knitting in the round over any other kind of knitting due to this continuity.

knitting in the round on double-pointed needles • When you are knitting in the round on a number of stitches too small to fit comfortably around a circular needle, you must use double-pointed needles. Double-pointed needles come in different lengths. I prefer to use 7-inch needles and a set of four needles. Certain lengths of needles are better suited for certain projects. You'll have to experiment to find a length that feels good to you.

Some projects call for double-pointed needles right away, on the cast-on row, and other projects transfer onto double-pointed needles as the stitches decrease in number. I will describe both types of situations, but for the purpose of this collection, you will mostly use double-pointed needles to finish the decrease rounds at the top of the hats. To do so, you will use four double-pointed needles, with the stitches being divided on three needles and the fourth needle being used to knit onto.

• Following are the steps for using four double-pointed needles at the top of a hat:

1. With the left circular needle in your left hand, begin knitting onto the first double-pointed needle. Knit as many stitches onto the first needle as directed in the pattern. Switch to the second double-pointed needle, which is empty, and begin knitting the required number of stitches onto this needle, being sure to pull the yarn snugly when transferring to this new needle. Do the same for the third needle. The three double-pointed needles form a triangle with the first and last stitches meeting at the beginning of the round.

   TIP • Some patterns will tell you how many stitches to put on each needle. Others will tell you to divide the stitches evenly onto three or four needles, and this is where that calculator can come in handy.

2. Be sure to keep track of the beginning of your round. Using a stitch marker becomes tricky with double-pointed needles because the marker can easily slip off the needle. I prefer to use a safety pin pinned directly to the knitting or a stitch marker that attaches to the completed knitted stitch. Figure out which marker works best for you.

   TIP • If you still want to use a ring marker, place the marker after the first stitch. Then remember that the stitch marker is placed after the first stitch in the round.

3. Begin knitting in the round just as you would with circular needles. Hold the first needle in your left hand, ready to knit. Hold the empty fourth needle in your right hand. This fourth needle is your working needle. Concentrate only on the needle you are knitting from and the working needle, basically ignoring the other needles. Insert the right needle into the first stitch on the left needle and knit as usual. Knit all the stitches on the first needle. When this needle is empty, it becomes your working needle.

   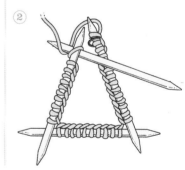

4. Hold the second needle in your left hand with the stitches ready to knit. Begin knitting the stitches onto the empty needle in your right hand. Knit all of the stitches on the second needle onto the working needle in your right hand. Make sure you pull the yarn snugly when starting a new needle so you don't create gaps along the way.

5. Knit across the stitches on the third and final needle to complete one round.

• Continue knitting in the round this way and decrease stitches as the pattern directs.

knitting in the round on double-pointed needles from the cast-on row

• This type of knitting with double-pointed needles is used often, especially when knitting smaller tubes, as for socks. For this collection, it is used in the Cherry-O! pattern.

1. Cast on all required stitches onto one double-pointed needle.

2. Knit the first round onto the double-pointed needles, dividing the stitches evenly onto three needles.

3. Hold the three needles so they form a triangle, with the first and last stitches meeting at the beginning of the round and the working yarn coming from the right needle.

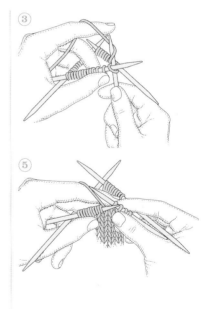

4. *Most important,* check to make sure the cast-on stitches are not twisted around any of the needles before you begin knitting.

5. With the empty fourth needle held in your right hand, insert the point into the first stitch on the first needle, which is held in your left hand. Focus only on the two working needles at a time, ignoring the other needles. Knit as usual until all stitches are knit from the first needle. Now empty, it becomes your working needle.

6. Work the same way across the other two needles, being sure to pull the yarn snugly when transferring from one needle to the next.

7. After completing one round, place a marker to show the beginning of the round. I prefer using a safety pin pinned directly the completed knitting, but you can use a ring stitch marker as well. Just place the ring marker after the first stitch so it doesn't slip off the needle.

• Continue knitting in the round as your pattern directs.

The knitting becomes easier after several rounds have been completed. Knitting with double-pointed needles can appear to be complicated and awkward, but once you understand the concept and you complete a few rounds, it will become easier for you.

I have taught many students to knit in the round at my hat classes, and they are never prouder than when they learn this technique. Their concentration is immense, but their feeling of accomplishment is even greater. I had one student shout out, "I can't believe I'm doing this!" as she knitted with double-pointed needles for the first time. The students' excitement makes me smile.

BINDING OFF

basic bind off • When you get to the end of a project or piece, and you want to remove it from the needles, you use a technique called binding off. It is far simpler than casting on, and new knitters are pleasantly surprised at how easy this step is. One problem to be aware of is binding off too tightly. This becomes a problem on projects such as sweaters, where necklines can be bound off so tightly that the sweater will literally not fit over the head of the wearer. There is an easy remedy for this. Simply bind off using a needle that is two sizes larger than the needle you are currently using. Hold this larger needle in your right hand and work the stitches onto this needle. If you don't use a larger needle, just make sure you are making a conscious effort to bind off loosely.

1. Knit 2 stitches onto the right needle.

2. Using the tip of your left needle, pass the right stitch on the right needle over the left stitch and off the needle. (I used to use my fingers to pick up the stitch and pass it over when I first started knitting.)

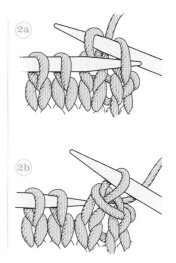

3. Knit the next stitch onto the right needle and repeat step 2.

• Repeat steps 2 and 3 until you have the desired number of bound-off stitches. You'll have 1 stitch remaining on your right needle. If you are at the end of a project or piece, cut your yarn, leaving a tail. Pull the tail through the last stitch and pull it up tight.

3-needle bind off • This type of bind-off is very slick. It is used in this collection for the top seam of several hats, but it can also be used for shoulder seams in sweaters. I like it because it eliminates the final step of seaming—you create a seam as you bind off. You'll see how easy it is!

TIP • Have an extra needle handy before you begin, as the title points out.

1. Turn the project inside out.

2. Divide the stitches evenly onto two needles and hold both of these needles parallel in your left hand. For this bind-off, you have to have the same number of stitches on each needle. The points of both needles are right next to each other and pointing to the right.

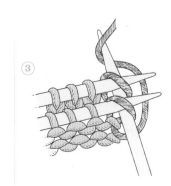

3. With the right (single) needle, knit through the first stitch on both needles and knit them together, making 1 stitch on the right needle. Repeat this so there are 2 stitches on the right needle.

4. On the right needle, pass the right stitch over the left stitch and off the needle.

5. Knit together through the next stitch on both left needles, making 1 more stitch on the right needle, and repeat step 4.

• Repeat steps 4 and 5 until 1 stitch remains on the right needle. Cut the yarn, leaving a tail, pull the tail through the last stitch, and pull it tight. Turn your project right side out and marvel at the beautiful seam you just made!

stitch notebook

Using different stitches creates different looks and textures in your knitting. Once you have the knit and purl stitches mastered, it is time to experiment with ways to combine these stitches. You will discover that certain stitches also make a piece look or behave a certain way. For example, stockinette stitch without a border stitch will roll up on all edges. Seed stitch and garter stitch will lie flat, making a perfect edging for a garment you don't want to have a rolled edge. Have fun learning about stitch patterns and how they can be used to enhance your knitting. You can practice these stitches first or learn as you go.

For each of the following stitch patterns, I have provided instructions for knitting back and forth, as well as in the round.

stockinette stitch

(worked over any number of stitches)

BACK AND FORTH

Row 1 (right side): Knit.
Row 2: Purl.
Repeat rows 1 and 2.

IN THE ROUND

Knit every round (knit side is the right side).

reverse stockinette stitch

(worked over any number of stitches)

BACK AND FORTH

Row 1 (right side): Purl.
Row 2: Knit.
Repeat rows 1 and 2.

IN THE ROUND

Purl every round (purl side is the right side).

garter stitch

(worked over any number of stitches)

BACK AND FORTH

Knit every row.

IN THE ROUND

Round 1: Knit.
Round 2: Purl.
Repeat rounds 1 and 2.

twisted stitch

(worked over an even number of stitches)

BACK AND FORTH

Row 1: Knit 1 stitch, knit in 2nd stitch on left needle and leave on left needle, knit in 1st stitch on left needle and slip both stitches onto right needle. Repeat to last stitch, knit 1 stitch.
Row 2: Purl.
Repeat rows 1 and 2.

IN THE ROUND

Round 1: Knit in 2nd stitch on left needle and leave on left needle, knit in 1st stitch on left needle and take both stitches off left needle. Repeat to end of round.
Round 2: Knit.
Repeat rounds 1 and 2.

seed stitch

(worked over an even number of stitches)

Row 1: Knit 1 stitch, purl 1 stitch. Repeat to end of row.
Row 2: Purl 1 stitch, knit 1 stitch. Repeat to end of row.
Repeat rows 1 and 2.

Round 1: Knit 1 stitch, purl 1 stitch. Repeat to end of round.
Round 2: Knit 1 stitch, purl 1 stitch. Repeat to end of round.
Repeat rounds 1 and 2.

basket weave

(worked over a multiple of 4 stitches)

Row 1: Knit 4 stitches, purl 4 stitches. Repeat to end of row.
Row 2: Knit 4 stitches, purl 4 stitches. Repeat to end of row.
Rows 3 and 4: Repeat rows 1 and 2.
Row 5: Purl 4 stitches, knit 4 stitches. Repeat to end of row.
Row 6: Purl 4 stitches, knit 4 stitches. Repeat to end of row.
Rows 7 & 8: Repeat rows 5 and 6.
Repeat rows 1–8.

Round 1: Knit 4 stitches, purl 4 stitches. Repeat to end of round.
Rounds 2–4: Repeat round 1.
Round 5: Purl 4 stitches, knit 4 stitches. Repeat to end of round.
Rounds 6–8: Repeat round 5.
Repeat rounds 1–8.

5x3 rib

(worked over a multiple of 8 stitches)

Row 1: Knit 5 stitches, purl 3 stitches. Repeat to end of row.
Row 2: Knit 3 stitches, purl 5 stitches. Repeat to end of row.
Repeat rows 1 and 2.

Knit 5 stitches, purl 3 stitches. Repeat to end of round and every following round.

simple cable pattern

(worked over a multiple of 6 stitches)

Row 1: Knit.
Row 2: Purl.
Row 3 (cable row): Place next 3 stitches on cable needle, hold cable needle to front, knit 3 stitches, knit 3 stitches from cable needle.
Rows 4–8: Work in stockinette stitch, starting with a purl row.
Row 9: Repeat row 3 (cable row).
Row 10: Purl.
Repeat rows 1–10.

Rounds 1 and 2: Knit.
Round 3 (cable round): Place next 3 stitches on cable needle, hold cable needle to front, knit 3 stitches, knit 3 stitches from cable needle.
Rounds 4–8: Knit.
Round 9: Repeat round 3 (cable round).
Round 10: Knit.
Repeat rounds 1–10.

technique notebook

Once you get the basic knit and purl stitches down, it is time to learn how to use these stitches in different ways. You will see how the following techniques all build on the skills you have already learned.

SLIPPING STITCHES

Slipping is used in several decreasing techniques, stitch patterns, and edgings. In a pattern, the instruction is usually written just as *slip*. It is a simple technique that involves sliding a stitch from the left to the right needle. There are two ways to slip.

1. **Slip as if to knit:** Insert the right needle into the stitch on the left needle as you would to knit it. Don't knit the stitch; just slide it onto the right needle.

2. **Slip as if to purl:** Insert the right needle into the stitch on the left needle as you would to purl it. Don't purl the stitch; just slide it onto the right needle.

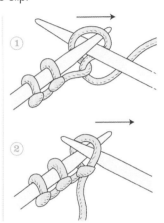

KNITTING THROUGH THE BACK

This terminology is used for making decreases and for different stitch patterns, and it will slant the stitch in a different direction. Usually you knit and purl through the *front* of a stitch, or "loop." When directed to knit or purl through the *back* loop, you do just that.

1. Knit through the back by inserting the right needle from right to left into the back of the stitch on the left needle. Then knit as usual.

2. Purl through the back by inserting the needle from left to right in the back, bringing the point to the front of the left needle. Then purl as usual.

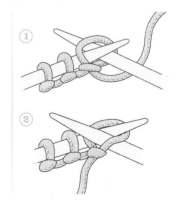

SHAPING

Shaping is a broader term that means decreasing and increasing while you are working. Shaping means that you make your knitted piece either narrower or wider at a certain point.

decreasing • Decreasing is used when you want to make your piece narrower at a certain point, like at the top of a hat. You do this by making fewer stitches as you go.

KNIT 2 STITCHES TOGETHER

This makes a right-slanting decrease.

1. With the right needle, and the yarn in back, put the point through the first 2 stitches on the left needle at the same time as if to knit.

2. Knit these 2 stitches together to make 1 stitch on the right needle.

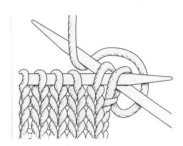

PURL 2 STITCHES TOGETHER

This makes a right-slanting decrease.

1. With the right needle, and the yarn in front, put the point through the first 2 stitches on the left needle at the same time as if to purl.

2. Purl these 2 stitches together to make 1 stitch on the right needle.

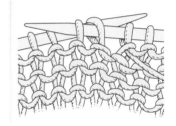

SLIP STITCH, SLIP STITCH, KNIT 2 STITCHES TOGETHER THROUGH THE BACK LOOPS, OR SLIP, SLIP, KNIT

This makes a left-slanting decrease.

1. With the right needle, and the yarn in back, slip the first 2 stitches, onto the right needle as if to knit.

2. With the left needle, put the point through the front of the 2 slipped stitches, on the right needle.

3. Knit the 2 slipped stitches together by wrapping the yarn around the right needle and pulling a loop through onto the right needle, making 1 stitch on the right needle.

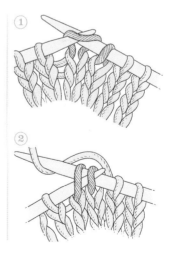

increases • Increases are used when you want to make your knitted piece wider. You do this by adding stitches as you go.

KNIT IN THE FRONT AND BACK OF THE SAME STITCH

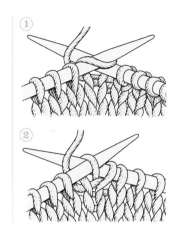

1. Knit the first stitch and leave it on the left needle.

2. Insert the tip of the right needle into the back of the same stitch and knit again.

3. Slip the stitch off the left needle. Two stitches have been made from 1 stitch and are now on the right needle.

PURL IN THE FRONT AND BACK OF THE SAME STITCH

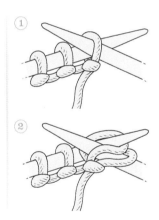

1. Purl the first stitch and leave it on the left needle.

2. Insert the tip of the right needle through the back of the same stitch from left to right and bring the point to the front. Purl again.

3. Slip the stitch off the left needle. Two stitches have been made from 1 stitch and are now on the right needle.

yarn overs • A yarn over is a way to add a stitch and leave a hole on purpose. In this book, yarn overs are used not only to increase but also to create eyelets.

YARN OVER COMING FROM A KNIT STITCH

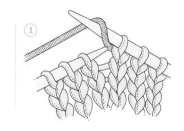

1. Bring the yarn to the front between the needles.

2. Wrap the yarn over the needle and to the back. Knit the next stitch.

1. The yarn is in the front.

2. Wrap the yarn over the needle and bring it back to the front. Purl the next stitch.

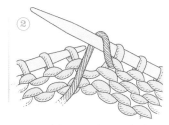

EYELETS

In this collection, eyelets are used in several places. They are used for tiny buttonholes, as holes for threading ribbon, and as a decorative turning row for a hem. They are made in two steps.

1. Knit to the point for the eyelet. Yarn over.

2. Knit the next 2 stitches together (see page 35). By knitting 2 stitches together after every yarn over, you'll keep the number of stitches consistent—you won't increase.

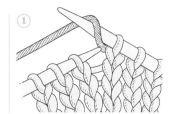

- Follow the directions for the next row or round when working the yarn over from the previous row. If the directions say nothing, just knit or purl the yarn over as you would a regular stitch. A tiny hole will be left, which is the eyelet.

PICK UP AND KNIT

Pick up and knit means that you will be picking up stitches along an edge or another place on the fabric as if you are going to knit them. This means you will insert the needle into your knitted fabric and wrap the yarn as if you are knitting. Put these new stitches on your right needle. You can use this technique for collars, edgings, and sleeves; in this book, you will mainly use it to create edgings. Be careful not to create holes as you are working by making sure you insert the needle into the correct point on the knitted piece. The pattern will tell you how many stitches to pick up.

1. With the yarn held to the back of your piece and the right side of your work facing you, take one needle in your right hand and insert the needle from front to back (right through the fabric) into each stitch just beneath the cast-on edge, or bind-off edge, or one stitch in on a side edge.

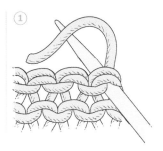

2. Wrap the yarn as if to knit and pull the loop through the fabric, leaving the new stitch on the right needle.

TIP • Many new knitters have trouble pulling the loop through the fabric once the yarn is wrapped around the needle. You can grab right onto the knitted fabric with your left fingers at the spot of insertion. Then move the fabric over the inserted needle in order to pull the yarn loop through and onto the needle.

If you are knitting back and forth, you will turn the piece and purl back (or follow the pattern stitch as directed in the pattern). If you are working in the round, you will join the ends and continue knitting or working the specified stitch. If you are picking up stitches to make an I-cord, you will use a double-pointed needle and slide the stitches to the other end and start knitting.

JOINING NEW COLORS

Joining a new color to start a stripe is done by holding the new color yarn in your left hand and beginning to knit with it. There is a little more to it than that, but not much. You will want to join the new color by tying it on to the old color on the wrong side of the fabric. Slide the knot up so it lies right behind the stitch you are going to knit with the new color. If you are

knitting back and forth, tie the new color on at the beginning of a row. If you are knitting in the round, twist the two colors around each other on the wrong side so you don't create a gap in the work. You will need to weave this end in when the piece is done.

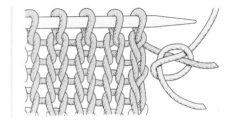

CARRYING COLORS

Carrying colors means you have more than one color active in your knitting at one time. You will need to carry the unused yarns along the wrong side of the fabric in a relaxed manner so the knitting won't pull or be distorted. When carrying colors up the work for stripes, my rule is not to carry them more than 5 rows. When carrying colors across the work for Fair Isle knitting (when motifs are knit right into the fabric),

my rule is not to carry over more than 4 stitches. When switching to a new color, be sure to twist the two colors around each other on the wrong side of the fabric so there isn't a gap in the work.

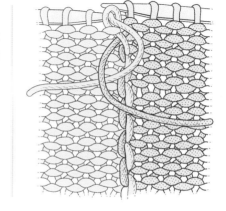

I-CORD

The I-cord has an interesting story behind it, and it begins with Elizabeth Zimmermann. She was one of the most beloved knitters in recent history, famous for her innovative and smart knitting. Her books are wonderful, and though instructive, they read like novels. Her sense of humor is sharp, and her view on knitting was that anyone can do it. When she came up with a new idea, she was certain someone else had thought of it already, so she would say she "unvented" it. Elizabeth Zimmermann "unvented" the I-cord, which is a simple technique used to make cords with two double-pointed needles. She thought this cording technique was so easy that she dubbed it "idiot" cord—I-cord for short. You will find that you will use this technique all the time. Here are the steps for making I-cord:

1. Using a double-pointed needle, cast on 2, 3, or 4 stitches depending how thick you want your cord. Knit these stitches using another double-pointed needle and do not turn the work.

2. Slide the stitches to the other end of the double-pointed needle. The yarn will now come from the last stitch.

3. Bring the yarn around the back and knit the stitches. Do not turn.

- Repeat rows 2 and 3 until the cord reaches the desired length. Bind off. Cut the yarn and pull it through the last stitch.

   TIP • When knitting I-cord, gently pull down on the cord as it forms. This helps you get the stitches to fall in place to better form the cord.

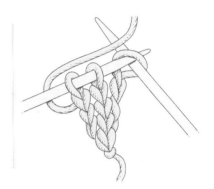

FINISHING

Finishing, in knitting terms, is basically anything you have to do—such as weaving in ends, sewing seams, or adding embellishments—to finish your project after the knitting is completed. It gives me great joy to finish projects, and I hope it will bring you the same satisfaction.

weaving in ends • Any ends or tails of yarn that are left from casting on, binding off, changing colors, or starting a new ball of yarn have to be woven into the knitted fabric. Do this by threading the end of a tail through a yarn needle. The wrong side of the piece should be facing you. Pull the yarn needle through the backs of 8–10 stitches, taking care that the yarn doesn't show on the right side. Cut the yarn, leaving about a ½-inch tail. On a seam, weave the end right into the seam. On the body of the fabric, weave horizontally and make sure your work doesn't show on the right side. Weave ends into matching colors to blend in better.

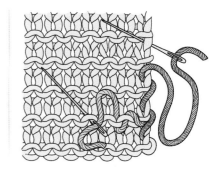

mattress stitch • The mattress stitch is the technique I mainly use for sewing seams in this book. Various seaming techniques are used for sewing different types of knit edges together, but they have the same principles as the mattress stitch. With the mattress stitch, you stitch with the right side of the fabric facing you, instead of turning everything inside out as in traditional sewing. I think having the right sides out makes it easier because you can see how it looks as you go. The mattress stitch is fairly straightforward and will be used again and again when you knit.

1. Lay the pieces flat with the right sides facing up. Pin the pieces together with safety pins if necessary. Thread a tail end or new piece of yarn through a yarn needle, and begin sewing at the bottom of the seam.

2. Working upward, find the bars or horizontal strands between the first stitch and second stitch up the sides of the pieces. You can do this by gently pulling apart the two stitches.

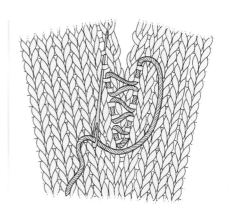

3. Put the needle under the first two bars on one side and draw the yarn through. Then place it under the two bars directly opposite on the other piece and draw the yarn through. Repeat back and forth this way, working up the seam two bars at a time on each side. As you go, be sure to insert the needle into the last "hole" you came out of on each side.

• Complete by weaving in the end along the seam on the inside of the piece.

whipstitch • You can also whipstitch two edges together, as for Chocolate Blues (page 136) and Snowman (page 159). It can be used as a decorative stitch on the right side of the fabric, or it can be used as an invisible seam on the wrong side of the fabric. Basically, you are wrapping the yarn around the outer edge of the fabric.

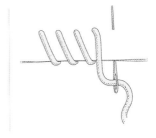

1. Line up pieces with either the right sides together or the wrong sides together. The pattern will tell you which way to put the fabric. You can pin the pieces together if you need to.

2. Work from right to left if you are completing a seam. Thread a tail end or new piece of yarn through a yarn needle. Holding the edges together, insert the needle 1 stitch in from the edge, from back to front, going through both pieces at the same time.

3. Pull the yarn through. Bring the needle around to the back side and insert it again in the next stitch.

• Repeat steps 2 and 3 as needed, then weave in the end.

sewing on an appliqué • Sewing on appliqués is not difficult and allows for some extra creativity. Knitted fabric is so pliable that you can create different shapes by stretching and molding the appliqué as you sew. When knitting the appliqués in this book, remember to leave a longer tail that can later be used for sewing the appliqué onto the hat.

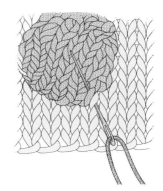

1. After placing appliqués by pinning them (onto the hat, in this case), begin by threading a tail end or piece of matching yarn onto a yarn needle.

2. Work around the outer edge of the appliqué, turning your work as you go. Pick up a stitch on the hat, sew through the outermost edge of the appliqué, and pull the yarn through. Repeat all the way around the appliqué.

3. Pull the end through to the inside, tie it off, and weave in the end.

TIP • To tie off an appliqué or the top of a hat, simply use the needle to pull the end of the yarn through to the inside of the hat. Then pull the yarn through a couple of loops on the inside of the hat, leaving a small loop close to the fabric. Put the needle through this loop and pull up gently until the knot is tight. Weave in the end for extra security.

crochet

Learning a few simple crochet techniques can add a lot to your knitting. I use crochet for edgings and embellishments for many of the hats in this collection. It is fun and it adds a fun twist to the projects.

SLIP KNOT

The slip knot is the very first step to begin crochet.

1. Measure out about 4 inches from the tail end of the ball of yarn. You will make a slip knot at this point on the yarn.

2. Make a loop, overlapping the yarn at the bottom of the loop.

3. Bring the yarn that is on top of the overlap behind and then through the loop, making another loop. Pull up.

4. Put the new loop on the hook and tighten it to fit.

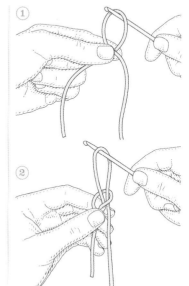

CHAIN STITCH

The chain stitch is the place to start when learning to crochet. With a slip knot on the hook, with the hook in your right hand, and with your left hand holding the working yarn as you would for Continental knitting (see page 23), continue as follows:

1. Wrap the yarn over the hook from back to front (counterclockwise).

2. Catching the yarn with your hook, pull it through the loop on the hook. (You may need to hold the slip knot with the thumb and middle finger of your left hand to keep it steady.)

• Repeat steps 1 and 2 until desired number of chain stitches are made.

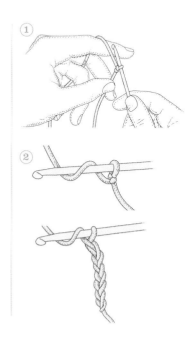

SLIP STITCH

The slip stitch is often used to join rounds when crocheting in a circle or when making a picot edging.

1. Insert the hook into the two upper strands of the appropriate stitch as directed in the pattern.

2. Wrap the yarn over the hook from back to front (counterclockwise) and pull it through the stitch.

3. With two loops on the hook, pull the second loop through the first loop.

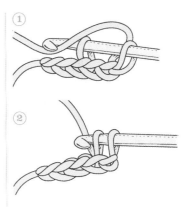

SINGLE CROCHET

The single crochet is one of the first stitches you'll need to learn. It is the most basic stitch, but it can be used to create almost anything.

1. Insert the hook into the two upper strands of the appropriate stitch as directed in the pattern.

2. Wrap the yarn over the hook from back to front (counterclockwise) and pull it through the stitch.

3. Wrap the yarn over the hook once more and pull it through both loops.

• Repeat as directed.

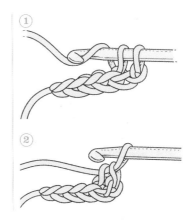

embroidery

Embroidering your finished knitted piece can add a big dose of character to your work. From simple outlining to more dramatic stitching, you can create fabulous detail for your piece with embroidery. Always use a cut piece of yarn no longer than 18 inches and a yarn needle. The following techniques are used in this collection.

BACKSTITCH

The backstitch is used to make lines that are straight or curved. Make the stitches small and as even as possible.

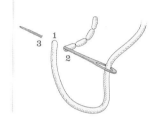

1. Cut a length of yarn and thread it on a yarn needle. Pull the yarn through several loops on the wrong side of the fabric, leaving a ½-inch tail. With the needle, pull the yarn through to the right side at your starting point.

2. Moving backward from your starting point, insert your needle at 2 and have the point of the needle come out at 3. This should be one motion.

3. Pull the yarn through, insert the needle into the new 1, and have the point of the needle come out at 4.

   - Keep working in this way, moving backward and forward, until you have completed the length of stitching desired. At the last stitch, pull the yarn through to the back and weave in the end on the wrong side of the knitted fabric.

SATIN STITCH

The satin stitch is used to fill in spaces and to create a certain shape. It is worked in one motion and moves quickly.

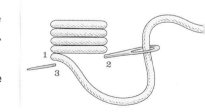

1. Cut a length of yarn and thread it on a yarn needle. Pull the yarn through several loops on the wrong side of the fabric. Pull the needle through to the right side, at the starting point.

2. Insert the needle at 2 and have the point of the needle come out at 3. Pull the yarn through.

   - Repeat step 2 until the space is filled. On the last stitch, pull the yarn through to the wrong side of the knitted fabric and weave in the end.

STRAIGHT STITCH

The straight stitch is used in this collection to create a decorative border around holes knitted into the fabric, for example, in the Reversible Stripes and Dots hat on page 121. It brings attention and color to the textural interest of the fabric.

1. Cut a length of yarn and thread it on a yarn needle. Pull the yarn through several loops on the wrong side of the fabric. Pull the needle through to the open middle of the knitted hole. This is the starting point.

2. Insert the needle at 2 and bring the needle back through the open middle. Pull the yarn through.

3. Insert the needle at 3 and bring the needle back through the open middle. Pull the yarn through.

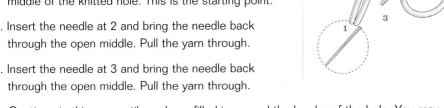

- Continue in this way until you have filled in around the border of the hole. You may have to overlap the stitches somewhat to get a solid look. Don't worry if all of the stitches are not the exact same length; this adds more character. Mine aren't and probably never will be.

RUNNING STITCH

The running stitch can be decorative or can be used as a seaming stitch. I always think of it as an over-under stitch, sort of like a dotted line. In this book, the running stitch is used to attach the snowman's scarf to the hat, for example, in the Snowman hat on page 159.

1. Cut a length of yarn and thread it on a yarn needle. Pull the yarn through several loops on the wrong side of the fabric. Pull the yarn through to the right side. This is your starting point.

2. Insert the needle at 2 and bring it up at 3, pulling the yarn through in one motion.

3. Insert the needle at 4 and bring it up at 5, pulling the yarn through in one motion.

- Repeat to the end of the desired length. Pull the yarn through to the wrong side of the knitted fabric. Weave in the end.

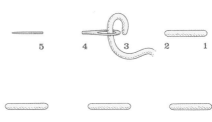

FRENCH KNOT

I love using French knots as a decorative stitch on my knitting. However, my French knots, when done exactly according to directions, never turn out quite right. So here is my own twist on this technique.

1. Cut a length of yarn and thread it on a yarn needle. Pull the yarn through several loops on the wrong side of the fabric. Pull the yarn through to the right side of the fabric. This will place the French knot.

2. Wrap the yarn around the needle three times while holding the needle close to the fabric. Hold the yarn wraps taut by pinching the yarn between your left thumb and index finger. Insert the needle nearby and pull it gently through to wrong side of the fabric.

3. Insert the needle right next to the wraps and pull the yarn through to the right side of the fabric.

4. Insert the needle into the center of the knot just created and pull it through to the wrong side of the fabric. This extra stitch makes the French knot much more secure and gives it a finished look.

- If you are making one knot, cut the yarn and weave in the end. If you are making many knots, you can carry the yarn over the back of your work to the different spots only if you can't see the carried yarn through the fabric. If you can see it from the right side, you'll have to cut your yarn and tie it off for each French knot, then reattach the yarn at the new spots as you go.

poms, tassels, and fringe

Pompons—or poms, as I like to call them—tassels, and fringe are staples in hat making for children. To make them easily and uniformly, consider picking up a Pom Tree (see page 13), but if you can't, some cardboard will do. Let's get started.

POMS

You will need cardboard strips cut to the width the pattern requires, scissors, and a yarn needle to attach the pom. You can use different widths and wraps to create different looks.

For example, a pattern in this book might tell you to make a 2-inch pom with 40 wraps. You do this as follows:

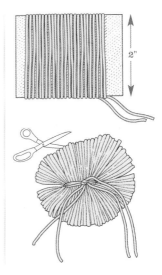

1. Cut a 2-inch strip of cardboard or set the Pom Tree pegs at 2 inches.

2. Wrap the yarn around the cardboard or pegs 40 times and cut the end.

3. Tie an 8-inch length of yarn tightly around the center of the wrapped yarn using a double knot (tie the yarn as if you were beginning to tie your shoe, then do it again). The cardboard needs to be carefully pulled from the center before doing this, as you need to tie all the way around the wrapped yarn. If you are using the Pom Tree, slide the wrapped and tied yarn off the pegs.

    TIP • I have a great trick for tying a knot without the extra finger needed to keep it from slipping. Use a surgical knot. When you are making the double knot, bring the yarn under twice instead of just once and pull up tight. This extra time under keeps the knot from slipping before you make the second half of your knot. I learned this trick from a knitting friend and later found out it was a surgical knot when I was instructing a physician friend of mine.

4. Slide your scissors into the loops and snip, making sure you cut through all of the loops.

5. Give the pom a trim. You can clean up the shape by trimming the uneven ends.

• Attach the pom by threading the ends from the tie onto a yarn needle and pulling the ends through to the inside of the hat. Secure the pom with a few small stitches inside the hat, then weave in the ends.

TASSELS

Tassels are used for a dangly, fringy embellishment, but I also like to attach them so they stand straight up. Again, the Pom Tree works great here, but cardboard works, too. You will need scissors and a yarn needle as well.

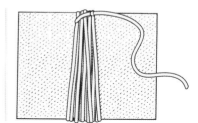

1. Cut a piece of cardboard to the width directed in the pattern or set the pegs on the Pom Tree to that width.

2. Wrap the yarn the desired number of times around the cardboard or pegs.

3. Thread an 8-inch length of yarn on a yarn needle and slide it through the middle of the wrapped yarn. Tie with a double knot at the top of the wrapped yarn (see the tip on page 47 for a no-slip knot). If making a tassel with cardboard, gently remove the wrapped yarn from the cardboard at this time.

4. With another 8-inch length of yarn, wrap around all of the loops about a third of the way from the top of the tassel and tie using a double knot. You can wrap around the tie more than once for extra support on a larger tassel. Leave these ends long for now. If you are usnig a Pom Tree, slide the tassel off it at this time.

5. Slide your scissors in the loops and snip. Trim all uneven ends. Take the loose ends from the tie, pull them under the wrapped yarn, and pull them through to the center of the tassel. Trim these to match the rest of the tassel.

6. Attach the tassel to that hat by running the ends left at the top of the tassel through to the inside of the hat. Tie the ends and weave them into the inside of the hat. You can make the tassel stand straight up by taking one of the ends from the tie and sewing the top of the tassel directly to the hat in an upright position.

Fringe is usually applied to the edges of knitted pieces, but it can be put in other places as well. The Pom Tree can be used to cut lengths of yarn very quickly, or you can wrap the yarn around cardboard, a book, or a notepad. You will need a crochet hook and scissors as well.

1. Cut the yarn to the length and the number of pieces desired.

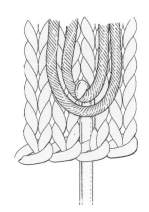

2. Holding 2 strands of yarn (or the desired number) together, fold them in half.

3. Lay the knitted fabric on a table in front of you. Insert the crochet hook through the fabric from back to front and under 2 loops of the stitch on the edge. This will provide more support for the fringe.

4. Insert the crochet hook into the loop end of the folded strands and pull the strands halfway through the stitch.

5. Pull the cut ends through their own loops with the crochet hook. Tighten the fringe by gently pulling the cut ends. Trim if necessary.

ties and flaps

Your baby is either a hat person or not. If yours is the latter, there is hope. You can add ties, ear flaps, or both to any of these hats, increasing the chances that it will stay on a baby who doesn't want to wear a hat. Try the options I've given here. Then tie the hat on securely and cross your fingers!

MARKERS FOR PLACEMENT

1. This is the first step for all ties and flaps. Find the back center of the hat and mark it with a safety pin.

2. Measure about 3 inches from the back to one side of the hat and place a safety pin.

• Repeat on the other side.

> TIP • The 3 inches can vary slightly due to the size of the hat, so adjust as needed. If you have a rolled-brim hat, let the edge roll naturally and attach the ties just inside the roll. This way, the tie doesn't distort the original shape of the hat.

SKINNY BRAIDED TIES

1. Cut 6 strands of yarn 36 inches long.

2. Thread 3 strands on a yarn needle and pull them through the spot marked for placement until the ends are even.

3. You will now have 6 strands that are 18 inches long. Divide the strands into three groups of 2 strands each.

4. Braid the strands, leaving 2 inches at the end. Tie a knot to secure the braid and trim the ends even.

• Repeat on the other side.

THICK BRAIDED TIES

1. Cut 12 strands of yarn 36 inches long. You will pull 6 strands through each side at the marked spots.

2. Thread 2 strands on a yarn needle and pull through the stitch at the marked spot until the ends are even.

3. Repeat with 2 more strands, pulling through the stitch directly next to the first. Repeat with 2 more strands, pulling through the stitch directly next to the second.

4. You will now have 12 strands that are 18 inches long. Divide these strands into three groups of 4 strands each. Braid the strands, leaving 2 inches at the end. Tie a knot to secure the braid and trim the ends even.

• Repeat on the other side.

I-CORD TIES

1. With double-pointed needles, pick up and knit (see page 37) 4 stitches at the marked spot on the side of the hat.

2. Using the I-cord technique (see page 39), work until cord measures 18 inches.

3. Bind off. Cut the yarn and pull it through the last stitch. Weave the end inside the cord. Tie a knot at the end for a more finished look.

• Repeat on the other side.

VARIATION • I-cord can be knitted with 2 or 3 stitches for skinnier ties.

OPTION • Add poms or tassels to the ends of the cord.

RIBBON TIES

1. Cut an 18-inch length of the selected ribbon.

2. Sew the ribbon with a needle and thread at the marked spot and to the inside of brim of the hat.

- Repeat on the other side.

EAR FLAPS

With a double-pointed needle and the appropriate-color yarn, pick up and knit (see page 37) 8 stitches on either side of the side marker (16 stitches total). On a rolled-brim hat, pick up stitches on the inside of the hat above the natural roll of the edge.

Turn your work and purl the next row using 2 double-pointed needles (used as straight needles to knit back and forth). Then work as follows:

Rows 1–8: Work in stockinette stitch (see page 32), starting with a knit row.
Row 9: Slip, slip, knit (see page 35); knit 12 stitches; knit 2 stitches together. 14 stitches remain.
Row 10: Purl.
Row 11: Knit.
Row 12: Purl.
Row 13: Slip, slip, knit; knit 10 stitches, knit 2 stitches together. 12 stitches remain.
Row 14: Purl 2 stitches together, purl 8 stitches, purl 2 stitches together. 10 stitches remain.
Row 15: Slip, slip, knit; knit 6 stitches; knit 2 stitches together. 8 stitches remain.
Row 16: Bind off the last 8 stitches. Cut the yarn and weave the end inside the ear flap.

Repeat on the other side.

VARIATION • Use other stitches such as garter stitch or seed stitch, for ear flaps that will lay flatter, or use a stitch that matches the hat.

EAR FLAPS AND TIES

Knit ear flaps onto the hat, then add any of the ties on pages 50–51 to the ear flaps. Place the ties at the center of the bottom row of the flaps. You may want to shorten the ties by a couple of inches to compensate for the length of the ear flaps.

start simple

If you haven't knitted a hat in the round before, this is the place to start. The following three hat patterns show you how to make a plain rolled-brim baby hat using three different yarn weights. The pattern is basically exactly the same for all three hats. The only differences are the gauge, the size of the needles used, and a slight variance in sizing. Everything else is done the same throughout.

There are also patterns for three easy ways to put a topper on these hats to add some character if you so choose. These toppers require no extra knitting and look fantastic.

Let's get started knitting, and I promise you will become as addicted to making these small hats as I am.

simple baby cap 1

If you are making your first hat, then definitely begin with this pattern. Here is the no-frills, rolled-brim baby hat that every beginner can quickly master. Briefly read through the pattern and note the skills needed. If you haven't used these skills yet, you can learn them as you go along. Go ahead and dive in. Start a real project. It is much more motivating to be making something wonderful than to be knitting a practice square.

skills needed

- Long-tail cast-on (page 20)
- Knit stitch (page 23)
- Knitting in the round on circular needles (page 26)
- Knit 2 stitches together (page 35)
- Knitting in the round on double-pointed needles (page 27)

size

- Newborn (0–6 months, 6–12 months, 1–2 years)

> TIP • All of the directions are written with the newborn size first, with the other sizes written in the above order in parentheses. Remember to follow the same size instructions throughout the pattern.

yarn

- DK or light worsted-weight yarn (110 yds)

  Sample was made with Rowan Handknit Cotton (100% cotton; 93 yards/50 grams), 1 skein #253 Tope

> TIP • When first trying a new pattern, it is best to use the suggested yarn. This will give you the best chance for duplicating the hat as it is in the photo. I selected the yarn for each pattern with a specific purpose and look in mind. If you choose to substitute another yarn, just make sure it is the same weight to achieve the correct gauge. If you are not sure about this, ask an experienced knitter or an employee where you shop for the yarn.

tools

- 16-inch circular needles, U.S. size 7 or size needed to obtain gauge
- Set of 4 double-pointed needles, U.S. size 7 or size needed to obtain gauge
- Stitch marker
- Ruler or tape measure
- Scissors
- Yarn needle

gauge

- 5 stitches per inch

HAT

With circular needles, use the long-tail method (page 20) to cast on 64 (72, 80, 88) stitches. The following steps will start you knitting in the round.

1. Spread the stitches out around the circular needle with the first and last stitches meeting at the points of the needles. Be sure the working yarn is coming from the right needle.

2. Place a stitch marker to show the beginning of the round by slipping a stitch marker onto your right needle before you begin knitting.

3. **Most important,** be careful that the stitches are not twisted on the circular needles before you make that first stitch connecting the ends. You only have to worry about this one time: before you connect the circle together. After this first stitch, you don't have to think about twisted stitches again.

4. Join to make a circle by knitting into the first stitch on the left needle. Continue knitting every stitch to the end of the round.

Knit every round until the hat measures 5½ (6, 6½, 7), inches from the cast-on edge. Measure by placing a ruler at the cast-on edge and measuring to the row just below your needle. Let the knitted fabric relax, and don't pull or stretch it while measuring the length. When you reach the desired length for the size hat you are making, you are ready to begin the decrease sequence.

> TIP • This hat is meant to roll up at the bottom. The rolled edge happens naturally when knitting in stockinette stitch (knitting every round), but sometimes the edge needs a little coaxing to get the roll going. Do this by putting your left hand inside the hat. Place the bottom edge of the hat on your left palm facing you, and gently force the edge to roll up using your right hand. Continue rolling the edge up in this way around the entire cast-on edge. You can do this while the hat is still on the needles, or you can wait until you are finished. I like to roll the edge while I am knitting so I get a feel for how the finished hat is going to look.

decrease sequence

The decrease sequence is a series of rounds to make the hat close up neatly and form the lines on the top of the hat. The tidy-looking lines are naturally created by knitting 2 stitches together in the following sequence.

Round 1: Knit 6 stitches, knit 2 stitches together. Repeat to the end of the round. 56 (63, 70, 77) stitches remain.

Round 2: Knit 5 stitches, knit 2 stitches together. Repeat to the end of the round. 48 (54, 60, 66) stitches remain.

Round 3: Knit all stitches.

Round 4: You will begin knitting this round with the double-pointed needles, as you will soon have too few stitches to fit on the circular needles. Do this by knitting directly onto 3 of the double-pointed needles as follows:

Needle 1: Knit 4 stitches, knit 2 stitches together. Repeat 3 (3, 3, 4) times. 15 (15, 15, 20) stitches are on the first needle.

Needle 2: Knit 4 stitches, knit 2 stitches together. Repeat 3 (3, 3, 4) times. 15 (15, 15, 20) stitches are on the second needle.

Needle 3: Knit 4 stitches, knit 2 stitches together. Repeat 2 (3, 4, 3) times. 10 (15, 20, 15) stitches are on the third needle. 40 (45, 50, 55) total stitches remain.

Use the fourth, or free, double-pointed needle to knit the stitches on each needle for the following rounds.

Round 5: Knit all stitches.

Round 6: Knit 3 stitches, knit 2 stitches together. Repeat to the end of the round. 32 (36, 40, 44) stitches remain.

Rounds 7 and 8: Knit all stitches.

Round 9: Knit 2 stitches, knit 2 stitches together. Repeat to the end of the round. 24 (27, 30, 33) stitches remain.

Round 10: Knit all stitches.

Round 11: Knit 1 stitch, knit 2 stitches together. Repeat to the end of the round. 16 (18, 20, 22) stitches remain.

Round 12: Knit 2 stitches together. Repeat to the end of the round. 8 (9, 10, 11) stitches remain.

Cut the yarn, leaving a 6-inch tail, and thread the tail onto a yarn needle. Thread each stitch onto the yarn needle and off the knitting needles. Pull the tail through the remaining stitches. Pull tightly to completely close the ring. Secure the yarn on the inside of the hat by weaving in the end through several stitches. Trim the excess yarn close to the hat. Weave in the end at the brim of the hat along the cast-on edge so it is hidden in the roll.

simple baby cap 2

This hat is knit in a slightly heavier weight yarn but follows the same pattern. You can achieve different looks just by this slight variation in yarn. Here your gauge is set at $4^{1}/_{2}$ stitches per inch.

skills needed

- Long-tail cast-on (page 20)
- Knit stitch (page 23)
- Knitting in the round on circular needles (page 26)
- Knit 2 stitches together (page 35)
- Knitting in the round on double-pointed needles (page 27)

size

- Newborn (0–6 months, 6–12 months, 1–2 years, 2 years and up)

yarn

- Worsted-weight yarn (110 yds)
  Sample was made with GGH Samoa (50% cotton/50% microfiber; 104 yards/ 50 grams), 1 skein #91 (light blue)

tools

- 16-inch circular needles, U.S. size 7 or size needed to obtain gauge
- Set of 4 double-pointed needles, U.S. size 7 or size needed to obtain gauge
- Yarn needle
- Stitch marker
- Ruler or tape measure
- Scissors
- Yarn needle

gauge

- $4^{1}/_{2}$ stitches per inch

HAT

With circular needles, use the long-tail method to cast on 56 (64, 72, 80, 88) stitches. Slip a stitch marker onto the right needle to mark the beginning of the round. Join to make a circle for knitting in the round, being careful not to twist the stitches. Knit every round until the hat measures 5 (5½, 6, 6½, 7) inches from the cast-on edge. Next, begin the decrease sequence for the top of the hat.

decrease sequence

Round 1: Knit 6 stitches, knit 2 stitches together. Repeat to the end of the round. 49 (56, 63, 70, 77) stitches remain.
Round 2: Knit 5 stitches, knit 2 stitches together. Repeat to the end of the round. 42 (48, 54, 60, 66) stitches remain.
Round 3: Knit all stitches.
Round 4: Knit directly onto 3 of the double-pointed needles as follows:
Needle 1: Knit 4 stitches, knit 2 stitches together. Repeat 2 (3, 3, 3, 4) times. 10 (15, 15, 15, 20) stitches are on the first needle.
Needle 2: Knit 4 stitches, knit 2 stitches together. Repeat 2 (3, 3, 3, 4) times. 10 (15, 15, 15, 20) stitches are on the second needle.
Needle 3: Knit 4 stitches, knit 2 stitches together. Repeat 3 (2, 3, 4, 3) times. 15 (10, 15, 20, 15) stitches are on the third needle. 35 (40, 45, 50, 55) total stitches remain.

Use the fourth, or free, double-pointed needle to knit the stitches on each needle for the following rounds.
Round 5: Knit all stitches.
Round 6: Knit 3 stitches, knit 2 stitches together. Repeat to the end of the round. 28 (32, 36, 40, 44) stitches remain.

Rounds 7 and 8: Knit all stitches.
Round 9: Knit 2 stitches, knit 2 stitches together. Repeat to the end of the round.
21 (24, 27, 30, 33) stitches remain.
Round 10: Knit all stitches.
Round 11: Knit 1 stitch, knit 2 stitches together. Repeat to the end of the round.
14 (16, 18, 20, 22) stitches remain.

Round 12: Knit 2 stitches together. Repeat to the end of the round. 7 (8, 9, 10, 11) stitches remain.

Cut the yarn, leaving a 6-inch tail, thread the tail onto a yarn needle, and pull it through the remaining stitches. Pull tightly to completely close the ring. Weave in the end on the inside of the hat. Weave in the end on the brim of the hat.

simple baby cap 3 *

This hat is knit in a heavier weight yarn than Caps 1 and 2, but it follows along the same pattern again. The Manos del Uruguay yarn used to knit this sample is a thick-and-thin yarn, and it creates a very different look. Here your gauge is set at 4 stitches per inch. Be sure to check the needle size and gauge before you begin.

skills needed

- Long-tail cast-on (page 20)
- Knit stitch (page 23)
- Knitting in the round on circular needles (page 26)
- Knit 2 stitches together (page 35)
- Knitting in the round on double-pointed needles for the top of a hat (page 27)

size

- Newborn (0–6 months, 6–24 months, 2 years and up)

yarn

- Heavy worsted-weight yarn (110 yds) Sample was made with Manos del Uruguay (100% wool; 138 yards/100 grams), 1 skein #28 (dark pink)

tools

- 16-inch circular needles, U.S. size 9 or size needed to obtain gauge
- Set of 4 double-pointed needles, U.S. size 9 or size needed to obtain gauge
- Stitch marker
- Ruler or tape measure
- Scissors
- Yarn needle

gauge

- 4 stitches per inch

* For a striped, feather-topped version of this hat, see the photograph in column 2 on page 61.

HAT

With circular needles, use the long-tail method to cast on 48 (56, 64, 72) stitches. Slip a stitch marker onto the right needle to mark the beginning of the round. Join to make a circle for knitting in the round, being careful not to twist the stitches. Knit every round until the hat measures 4½ (5½, 6, 7) inches from the cast-on edge. Next, begin the decrease sequence for the top of the hat.

decrease sequence

Round 1: Knit 6 stitches, knit 2 stitches together. Repeat to the end of the round. 42 (49, 56, 63) stitches remain.

Round 2: Knit 5 stitches, knit 2 stitches together. Repeat to the end of the round. 36 (42, 48, 54) stitches remain.

Round 3: Knit all stitches.

Round 4: Knit directly onto 3 of the double-pointed needles as follows:

Needle 1: Knit 4 stitches, knit 2 stitches together. Repeat 2 (2, 3, 3) times. 10 (10, 15, 15) stitches are on the first needle.

Needle 2: Knit 4 stitches, knit 2 stitches together. Repeat 2 (2, 3, 3) times. 10 (10, 15, 15) stitches are on the second needle.

Needle 3: Knit 4 stitches, knit 2 stitches together. Repeat 2 (3, 2, 3) times. 10 (15, 10, 15) stitches are on the third needle. 30 (35, 40, 45) total stitches remain.

Use the fourth, or free, double-pointed needle to knit the stitches on each needle for the following rounds.

Round 5: Knit all stitches.

Round 6: Knit 3 stitches, knit 2 stitches together. Repeat to the end of the round. 24 (28, 32, 36) stitches remain.
Rounds 7 and 8: Knit all stitches.
Round 9: Knit 2 stitches, knit 2 stitches together. Repeat to the end of the round. 18 (21, 24, 27) stitches remain.
Round 10: Knit all stitches.
Round 11: Knit 1 stitch, knit 2 stitches together. Repeat to the end of the round. 12 (14, 16, 18) stitches remain.

Round 12: Knit 2 stitches together. Repeat to the end of the round. 6 (7, 8, 9) stitches remain.

Cut the yarn, leaving a 6-inch tail, and thread the tail onto a yarn needle. Pull it through the remaining stitches. Pull tightly to completely close the ring. Weave in the end on the inside of the hat. Weave in the end on the brim of the hat.

three simple toppings

These quick and easy hat toppers are fun and look adorable on simple hats. Adding fleece, tulle, or feathers will give the hats a unique personality. Fleece is a great topper for all babies and adds to the soft lovability of the hat. Tulle always reminds me of ballet and the beloved tutu. And when you want a true show stopper, feathers are the way to go. Feathers, in particular, make people smile, and the little ones enjoy wearing the feathers on their heads. They won't shed if they are securely attached, but I suggest making the feather hat for children who are a little older, just to be safe.

The number of strips of fleece or tulle needed for these toppings depends on the number of stitches you cast on to start the hat. Read through the directions for the fleece and tulle toppings to see the length and width of the strips of fabric. Then cut the number of strips needed as follows:

Cast on 48 stitches—7 strips needed
Cast on 56 stitches—8 strips needed
Cast on 64 stitches—9 strips needed
Cast on 72 stitches—10 strips needed
Cast on 80 stitches—11 strips needed
Cast on 88 stitches—12 strips needed

Each strip, for both the tulle and the fleece, will be placed on a decrease line at the top of the hat. When you look at the top of the hat, you can see these stitch lines going out from the center circle. These lines are easier to see on knitted fabrics made of certain yarns than others, but they are the line of slightly raised knit stitches on the top of the hat. Thread one strip on a yarn needle and pull it through a stitch, going under both loops, an inch out from the center circle on a decrease stitch line. Continue placing the strips on the hat until there is one strip pulled through each decrease line. Pull the remaining strip through the center circle.

For finishing, follow the individual instructions for the fleece or tulle topping.

- Small amount of fleece
- Scissors
- Ruler or tape measure
- Yarn needle

Cut the fleece into 6-inch by 1-inch strips. Check the list on page 59 for the number of strips needed. Place the strips on the hat as previously directed. After all of the strips are on the hat, tie each strip in a half-knot and pull tight to secure. Next cut the 1-inch ends in half, the long way, to make four ½-inch strips coming from each knot.

- Tulle on a spool (available at craft and fabric stores, usually in bridal section)
- Scissors
- Ruler or tape measure
- Yarn needle

Cut the tulle into 20-inch strips. Check the list on page 59 to see the number of strips needed. Place the strips on the hat as directed on page 59. After all of the strips are placed, tie each strip in a bow, pulling tightly to secure. Separate the bow loops and fluff them up. Trim the ends at an angle for a more finished look.

- Feather boa (available at craft and fabric stores)
- Scissors
- Ruler or tape measure
- Sewing needle and thread

Cut an 8-inch piece of the boa. Wind the boa piece into a spiral to create a ball. With the needle and thread, sew the boa together, being sure to secure all layers together. The feathers are held in place with a skinny rope, and the needle and thread need to go through this rope. Sewing the boa can be difficult because you can't see exactly where to put the needle, so just feel as best you can, pulling gently at the boa as you go to check for any loose sections. Give the feather ball a good shake to dislodge any loose or flyaway feathers. Amazingly enough, the feathers won't shed much at all after the cutting, sewing, and shaking.

Using needle and thread again, sew the feathers to the top of the hat at the center circle, making sure to attach them securely. Tie off the thread and cut.

animals

Baby clothing is often associated with animals. These motifs are sweet, playful, and fun, just like babies. I enjoy taking traditional baby motifs and tweaking them slightly to make them work in the knitting world. The Bunny Tail pattern is simple in that it doesn't introduce any new techniques, but uses the skills acquired with the Simple Baby Caps in a slightly different way. You may want to start here if you are a new knitter.

Exciting new techniques are introduced with the other patterns in this section, including some easy crochet and appliqué ideas. Try to keep moving your knitting along by adding new techniques with every few projects. As you do, you add to the richness of your work. Don't become complacent with your knitting—try to keep growing. There is something for everyone and every baby in Animals, so run for the great outdoors and remember to take your knitting.

bunny tail

Babies in hats with ears are the best. I have made hats with ears added on after the hat is knit, but I wanted to design a pattern with the ears knit right on. So I came up with Bunny Tail. I have knitted this hat in every imaginable way, including using slightly textured yarns and even stripes (see page 62). I always add a tiny pom on the back of the hat for the bunny tail, but remember that babies nowadays spend most of their time on their backs. Make sure this pom is teeny-tiny so it won't bother the baby. When this hat is knitted in brown with shorter ears, it resembles a baby bear—with no bunny tail, of course.

skills needed

- Long-tail cast-on (page 20)
- Knit stitch (page 23)
- Knitting in the round on circular needles (page 26)
- Knitting 2 stitches together (page 35)
- Knitting in the round on double-pointed needles (page 27)
- Poms (page 47)

size

- Newborn (0–6, 6–12 months, 1–2 years)

yarn

- RYC Cashsoft Baby (57% extrafine merino wool/ 33% microfiber/10% cashmere; 142 yards/ 50 grams), 1 skein #800 Snowman

tools

- 16-inch circular needles, U.S. size 7 or size needed to obtain gauge
- Set of 4 double-pointed needles, U.S. size 7 or size needed to obtain gauge
- Stitch marker
- Ruler or tape measure
- Scissors
- Yarn needle
- 1 yard ribbon to tie around ears (optional)

gauge

- 5 stitches per inch

HAT

With circular needles, use the long-tail method to cast on 64 (72, 80, 88) stitches. Slip a stitch marker onto the right needle to mark the beginning of the round. Join to make a circle for knitting in the round, being careful not to twist the stitches. Knit every round until the hat measures 5½ (6, 6½, 7) inches from the cast-on edge. Next, begin the decrease sequence for the top of the hat.

decrease sequence

Round 1: Knit 6 stitches, knit 2 stitches together. Repeat to the end of the round. 56 (63, 70, 77) stitches remain.
Round 2: Knit 5 stitches, knit 2 stitches together. Repeat to the end of the round. 48 (54, 60, 66) stitches remain.
Round 3: Knit all stitches.
Round 4: Knit 4 stitches, knit 2 stitches together. Repeat to the end of the round. 40 (45, 50, 55) stitches remain.
Round 5: For newborn and 6–12 month sizes, knit all stitches. For sizes 0–6 months and 1–2 years, start this round by knitting the first 2 stitches together, then knit to the end of the round. 40 (44, 50, 54) stitches remain.

ears (each ear is worked separately)

Begin knitting the next round by knitting onto 3 of the double-pointed needles as follows:
Needle 1: Knit 7 (7, 8, 9) stitches onto the first needle.
Needle 2: Knit 7 (7, 8, 9) stitches onto the second needle.
Needle 3: Knit 6 (8, 9, 9) stitches onto the third needle.
Now half of the stitches are set to knit on double-pointed needles. Leave the other half of the stitches on the circular needle for now.

Working with the stitches on the double-pointed needles only, and using the fourth, or free, double-pointed needle, knit in the round, knitting every round, for 3 inches. Measure from the start of the ear to just below the needles.

Shape the top of the ear as follows: (If you have extra stitches at the end of the round, just knit them as directed.)
Round 1: Knit 2 stitches, knit 2 stitches together. Repeat to the end of the round. Knit 0 (2, 1, 3) stitches at the end of the round. 15 (17, 19, 21) stitches remain.
Round 2: Knit 1 stitch, knit 2 stitches together. Repeat to the end of the round. Knit 0 (2, 1, 0) stitches at the end of the round. 10 (12, 13, 14) stitches remain.
Round 3: Knit 2 stitches together. Repeat to the end of the round. Knit 0 (0, 1, 0) stitches at the end of the round. 5 (6, 7, 7) stitches remain.

Cut the yarn, leaving a 4-inch tail, thread the tail onto a yarn needle, and pull it through the remaining stitches. Weave in the end on the inside of the hat. Weave in the end on the brim of the hat.

Repeat the same directions for the second ear, transferring the stitches onto the double-pointed needles to begin.

making up

Sew the gap between the ears with the yarn needle and an 8-inch length of yarn. Make a crease in the ears by pinching the fabric together at the base and stitching it in place.
Optional: Tie ribbons into bows at the base of the ears.

tail

Make a 1-inch pom with 20 wraps for the tail and attach it to the back center of the hat just above the rolled brim.

speckled hen

I have a small ceramic hen and rooster collection, and most of them are hand-painted with polka dots and stripes. Recently, I have had my eye on a beautiful hen, speckled with black and white, at a local boutique. It reminds me of this hat. Its colors are obviously inspired by the black and white feathers, but I've created many versions of this hat inspired by different feathers I find. When you look for boas at your local craft or fabric stores, you'll be inspired by what you find as well. You can combine boas for different color combinations to go with the yarns of your choice. I usually make this hat for children who are a bit older because of the feathers, which can come loose.

skills needed

- Long-tail cast-on (page 20)
- Knit stitch (page 23)
- Knitting in the round on circular needles (page 26)
- Purl stitch (page 25)
- Knitting in the round on double-pointed needles (page 27)
- Knit 2 stitches together (page 35)

size

- 1–2 years (2 years and up)

yarn

- Rowan All Seasons Cotton (60% cotton/40% microfiber; 98 yards/50 grams), 1 skein each of #178 Organic and #182 Bleached
- Rowan Handknit Cotton (100% cotton; 93 yards/50 grams), 1 skein #252 Black

tools

- 16-inch circular needles, U.S. size 7 or size needed to obtain gauge
- Set of 4 double-pointed needles, U.S. size 7 or size needed to obtain gauge
- Stitch marker
- Ruler or tape measure
- Scissors
- Yarn needle

gauge

- 4½ stitches per inch

HAT

With circular needles and Organic, use the long-tail method to cast on 80 (88) stitches. Slip a stitch marker onto the right needle to mark the beginning of the round. Join to make a circle for knitting in the round, being careful not to twist the stitches. Knit every round until the hat measures 1½ inches from the cast-on edge. Next, begin the stripe pattern.

stripe pattern

Round 1: Knit with Black.
Round 2: Purl with Black.
Rounds 3–6: Knit with Bleached.
Rounds 7 and 8: Repeat rounds 1 and 2.
Rounds 9–12: Knit with Organic.
Repeat rounds 1–12 until the hat measures 6½ (7) inches from the cast-on edge. Next, begin the decrease sequence for the top of the hat using Bleached only.

decrease sequence

Round 1: Knit 6 stitches, knit 2 stitches together. Repeat to the end of the round. 70 (77) stitches remain.
Round 2: Knit 5 stitches, knit 2 stitches together. Repeat to the end of the round. 60 (66) stitches remain.
Round 3: Knit all stitches.
Round 4: Knit directly onto 3 of the double-pointed needles as follows:

Needle 1: Knit 4 stitches, knit 2 stitches together. Repeat 3 (4) times. 15 (20) stitches are on the first needle.

Needle 2: Knit 4 stitches, knit 2 stitches together. Repeat 3 (4) times. 15 (20) stitches are on the second needle.

Needle 3: Knit 4 stitches, knit 2 stitches together. Repeat 4 (3) times. 20 (15) stitches are on the third needle. 50 (55) total stitches remain.

Use the fourth, or free, double-pointed needle to knit the stitches on each needle for the following rounds.

Round 5: Knit all stitches.

Round 6: Knit 3 stitches, knit 2 stitches together. Repeat to the end of the round. 40 (44) stitches remain.

Rounds 7 and 8: Knit all stitches.

Round 9: Knit 2 stitches, knit 2 stitches together. Repeat to the end of the round. 30 (33) stitches remain.

Round 10: Knit all stitches.

Round 11: Knit 1 stitch, knit 2 stitches together. Repeat to the end of the round 20 (22) stitches remain.

Round 12: Knit 2 stitches together. Repeat to the end of the round. 10 (11) stitches remain.

Cut the yarn, leaving a 6-inch tail, thread the tail onto a yarn needle, and pull it through the remaining stitches. Pull tightly to completely close the ring. Weave in the ends on the inside of the hat.

feather topping

materials

- Feather boa (available at craft and fabric stores)
- Scissors
- Ruler
- Sewing needle and thread to match

Measure an 8-inch piece of the boa and cut. Wind the boa piece into a spiral to create a ball. With the needle and thread, sew the boa together, being sure to secure all layers together. The feathers are strung with a skinny rope, and the needle and thread need to go through this rope. Sewing the boa can be difficult because you can't see exactly where to put the needle, so just feel as best you can, pulling gently at the boa as you check for any loose sections. Give the feather ball a good shake to dislodge any loose or flyaway feathers. Amazingly enough, the feathers won't shed much after the cutting, shaking, and sewing.

Using the needle and thread again, sew the feathers to the top of the hat at the center circle, making sure to attach them securely.

painted turtle

Turtles remind me of going to northern Minnesota in the summers as a child. We used to see turtles by the lake all the time. The design of the shell has always intrigued me, and it is often colorful and very beautiful. Here, the little turtles are crocheted circles with colorful embroidery on top. Adding the turtles is a fun way to liven up this simple orange hat.

skills needed

* Long-tail cast-on (page 20)
* Knit stitch (page 23)
* Knitting in the round on circular needles (page 26)
* Knit 2 stitches together (page 35)
* Knitting in the round on double-pointed needles (page 27)
* Chain stitch (page 42)
* Single crochet (page 43)
* Slip stitch (page 43)
* Backstitch (page 44)
* Sewing on an appliqué (page 41)

size

* Newborn (0–6 months, 6–12 months, 1–2 years)

yarn

* Manos del Uruguay Cotton Stria (100% cotton; 116 yards/50 grams), 1 skein each of #206 (orange), #203 (dark green), and #204 (lime green)
* Small amounts of brightly colored yarn to embroider on turtle shells. The sample is done with Cotton Stria.

tools

* 16-inch circular needles, U.S. size 6 or size needed to obtain gauge
* Set of 4 double-pointed needles, U.S. size 6 or size needed to obtain gauge
* Stitch marker
* Ruler or tape measure
* Scissors
* Yarn needle
* Crochet hook, U.S. size E

gauge

* 5 stitches per inch

HAT

With circular needles and orange, use the long-tail method to cast on 64 (72, 80, 88) stitches. Slip a stitch marker onto the right needle to mark the beginning of the round. Join to make a circle for knitting in the round, being careful not to twist the stitches. Knit every round until the hat measures 5½ (6, 6½, 7) inches from the cast-on edge. Next, begin the decrease sequence for the top of the hat.

decrease sequence

Round 1: Knit 6 stitches, knit 2 stitches together. Repeat to the end of the round. 56 (63, 70, 77) stitches remain.

Round 2: Knit 5 stitches, knit 2 stitches together. Repeat to the end of the round. 48 (54, 60, 66) stitches remain.

Rounds 3 and 4: Knit all stitches.

Round 5: Knit directly onto 3 of the double-pointed needles as follows:

Needle 1: Knit 4 stitches, knit 2 stitches together. Repeat 3 (3, 3, 4) times. 15 (15, 15, 20) stitches are on the first needle.

Needle 2: Knit 4 stitches, knit 2 stitches together. Repeat 3 (3, 3, 4) times. 15 (15, 15, 20) stitches are on the second needle.

Needle 3: Knit 4 stitches, knit 2 stitches together. Repeat 2 (3, 4, 3) times. 10 (15, 20, 15) stitches are on the third needle. 40 (45, 50, 55) total stitches remain.

Use the fourth, or free, double-pointed needle to knit the stitches on each needle for the following rounds.

Rounds 6–8: Knit all stitches.

Round 9: Knit 3 stitches, knit 2 stitches together. Repeat to the end of the round. 32 (36, 40, 44) stitches remain.

Rounds 10 and 11: Knit all stitches.

Round 12: Knit 2 stitches, knit 2 stitches together. Repeat to the end of the round. 24 (27, 30, 33) stitches remain.

Round 13: Knit all stitches.

Round 14: Knit 1 stitch, knit 2 stitches together. Repeat to the end of the round. 16 (18, 20, 22) stitches remain.

Round 15: Knit all stitches.

Round 16: Knit 2 stitches together. Repeat to the end of the round. 8 (9, 10, 11) stitches remain.

Cut the yarn, leaving a 6-inch tail, thread the tail onto a yarn needle, and pull it through the remaining stitches. Pull tightly to completely close the ring. Weave in the ends on the inside of the hat.

crocheted turtle

(make 5 for newborn and 0–6 month-sizes, 6 for the larger sizes, in your choice of dark green and lime green)

With a crochet hook, chain 4 and join into a ring with a slip stitch.

Round 1: Work 6 single crochet into the center of the ring. Slip stitch to join the round.

Round 2: Chain 1 stitch. *Work 2 single crochet in the next stitch, 1 single crochet in the next stitch. Repeat from * to the end of the round. Slip stitch to join the round.

Round 3: Chain 1 stitch. *Work 2 single crochet in the next stitch, 1 single crochet in the next 2 stitches. Repeat from * to the end of the round. Slip stitch to join the round.

Round 4: Chain 1 stitch. *Work 2 single crochet in the next stitch, 1 single crochet in the next 3 stitches. Repeat from * to the end of the round. Slip stitch to join the round.

Round 5: Chain 1 stitch. *Work 2 single crochet in the next stitch, 1 single crochet in the next 4 stitches. Repeat from * to the end of the round. Slip stitch to join the round.

The following round makes the head, tail, and feet of the turtle.

Round 6: Chain 1, work 1 single crochet in the next stitch, slip stitch in the next stitch, chain 4, slip stitch in the same stitch.

Work 1 single crochet in the next 2 stitches, slip stitch in the next stitch, chain 4, slip stitch in the same stitch.

Work 1 single crochet in next the stitch, slip stitch in the next stitch, chain 5, slip stitch in the same stitch.

Work 1 single crochet in the next stitch, slip stitch in the next stitch, chain 4, slip stitch in the same stitch.

Work 1 single crochet in the next 2 stitches, slip stitch in the next stitch, chain 4, slip stitch in the same stitch.

Work 1 single crochet in the next stitch, slip stitch in the next stitch, chain 3 for tail.

Cut the yarn, leaving an 8-inch tail, and pull it through the remaining stitch (the loop on the hook).

making up

With brightly colored pieces of yarn and a yarn needle, sew markings to the back of the shell using the backstitch.

Pin the turtles to the hat, placing them randomly and alternating colors. Check placement, then sew them on with matching yarn and a yarn needle. The crocheted turtles naturally puff up a little; leave them like this while attaching them to the hat.

little chick

The chicks on this hat have motion with their legs and beaks. You can make just one chick or have a bunch running around the hat. The picot edge reminds me of a broken eggshell. I love the way this hat is sweet and fun at the same time.

- Long-tail cast-on (page 20)
- Knit stitch (page 23)
- Knitting in the round on circular needles (page 26)
- Purl stitch (page 25)
- Seed stitch (page 33)
- Knit 2 stitches together (page 35)
- Knitting in the round on double-pointed needles (page 27)
- Pick up and knit (page 37)
- Backward-loop cast-on (page 22)
- Bind off (page 30)
- Knit in the front and back of the same stitch (page 36)
- Sewing on an appliqué (page 41)
- Backstitch (page 44)

size

- Newborn (0–6 months, 6–12 months, 1–2 years)

yarn

- RYC Cashsoft Baby DK (57% extrafine merino wool/33% microfiber/10% cashmere; 142 yards/ 50 grams), 1 skein #800 Snowman
- GGH Samoa (50% cotton/50% microfiber; 104 yards/50 grams), 1 skein #5 Yellow
- Rowan Handknit Cotton (100% cotton; 93 yards/ 50 grams), small amounts of #309 Celery, #252 Black, and #254 Flame

tools

- 16-inch circular needle, U.S. size 7 or size needed to obtain gauge
- Set of 4 double-pointed needles, U.S. size 7 or size needed to obtain gauge
- Stitch marker
- Ruler or tape measure

- Scissors
- Yarn needle

gauge

- 5 stitches per inch

HAT

With circular needles and Snowman, use the long-tail method to cast on 64 (72, 80, 88) stitches. Slip a stitch marker onto the right needle to mark the beginning of the round. Join to make a circle for knitting in the round, being careful not to twist the stitches. Work in seed stitch for 4 rounds.
Knit until the hat measures 4½ (5, 5½, 6) inches from the cast-on edge. Next, begin the decrease sequence for the top of the hat.

decrease sequence

Round 1: Knit 6 stitches, knit 2 stitches together. Repeat to the end of the round. 56 (63, 70, 77) stitches remain.

Round 2: Knit 5 stitches, knit 2 stitches together. Repeat to the end of the round. 48 (54, 60, 66) stitches remain.

Round 3: Knit all stitches.

Round 4: Knit directly onto 3 of the double-pointed needles as follows:

Needle 1: Knit 4 stitches, knit 2 stitches together. Repeat 3 (3, 3, 4) times. 15 (15, 15, 20) stitches are on the first needle.

Needle 2: Knit 4 stitches, knit 2 stitches together. Repeat 3 (3, 3, 4) times. 15 (15, 15, 20) stitches are on the second needle.

Needle 3: Knit 4 stitches, knit 2 stitches together. Repeat 2 (3, 4, 3) times. 10 (15, 20, 15) stitches are on the third needle.
40 (45, 50, 55) total stitches remain.

Use the fourth, or free, double-pointed needle to knit the stitches on each needle for the following rounds.

Round 5: Knit all stitches.

Round 6: Knit 3 stitches, knit 2 stitches together. Repeat to the end of the round. 32 (36, 40, 44) stitches remain.

Rounds 7 and 8: Knit all stitches.

Round 9: Knit 2 stitches, knit 2 stitches together. Repeat to the end of the round. 24 (27, 30, 33) stitches remain.

Round 10: Knit all stitches.

Round 11: Knit 1 stitch, knit 2 stitches together. Repeat to the end of the round. 16 (18, 20, 22) stitches remain.

Round 12: Knit 2 stitches together. Repeat to the end of the round. 8 (9, 10, 11) stitches remain.

Cut the yarn; thread the tail onto a yarn needle. Pull it through the remaining stitches. Pull tightly to completely close the ring. Weave in the end at the cast-on edge to the inside of the hat.

picot edging

With circular needles and Snowman, pick up and knit 64 (72, 80, 88) stitches around the cast-on edge of the hat. Join and purl 1 round.

Round 2: Knit 1 stitch, slip stitch it onto left needle. *Cast on 2 backward-loop stitches. Bind off 4 stitches. Repeat from * across.

Cut the yarn, leaving a 6-inch tail, pull it through the remaining stitch, and weave in the tail on the inside of the hat.

chicks

(make 5 chicks for the first 2 sizes, 6 chicks for the 2 larger sizes)

body • Use 2 of the double-pointed needles as straight needles to knit back and forth. With Yellow, use the long-tail method to cast on 3 stitches.

Row 1: Knit in the front and back of the first stitch, knit 1 stitch, knit in the front and back of the last stitch. 5 stitches.

Row 2: Knit in the front and back of the first stitch, knit 3 stitches, knit in the front and back of the last stitch. 7 stitches.

Rows 3 and 4: Knit all stitches.

Bind off the remaining stitches. Cut the yarn, leaving a 6-inch tail. Pull it through the remaining stitch.

head • Use 2 of the double-pointed needles as straight needles to knit back and forth. With Yellow, use the long-tail method to cast on 3 stitches.

Rows 1–3: Knit all stitches.

Bind off. Cut the yarn, leaving a 6-inch tail. Pull it through the remaining stitch.

wing • Use 2 of the double-pointed needles as straight needles to knit back and forth. With yellow, use the long-tail method to cast on 3 stitches.

Row 1: Knit all stitches.

Row 2: Knit all stitches. Do not turn. Pass the 2nd and 3rd stitches over the 1st stitch.

Cut the yarn, leaving a 4-inch tail. Pull it through the remaining stitch.

making up

Using the seed stitch border as a guide, place and pin chicks (bodies and heads) evenly around the bottom of the hat. Using the tails and a yarn needle, sew the chicks in place. Sew the wings onto the bodies.

With Flame, use the backstitch to create feet and beaks. Make the feet going in different directions. With Black, make 1 small stitch for the eye. With Celery and the backstitch, make grass Vs randomly around the bottom.

from the garden

Inspiration pours into my knitting mind all day long, especially when I am outside. Pumpkins are an obvious place to start in this section. They are beautiful with their warm color, gentle texture, and round shape, kind of like a baby. The Little Pumpkin pattern will show you how to add texture to your knitting by throwing in a purl stitch every once in a while. The stem and leaf can be used to create any type of fruit or veggie hat you desire. Try a lemon, orange, peach, apple, blueberry, or tomato just by changing the color of the yarn. You could add texture stitches or simply knit every stitch for any of these hats. Become your own designer!

Flowers are a constant source of inspiration for me. The flower patterns in this section offer everything from a simple garter stitch strip rolled into a rosebud to a more complicated pattern with intricate petals and layers. The felted flower can be made separately to adorn your jean jacket, lapel, or handbag as well as your baby's hat. I'll warn you, though: You will be asked to make this flower for others when you wear it out and about. Again, start simple and then add to your repertoire to create your own inspiration. All you need is the determination to learn.

rosebud

Throughout the years, Rosebud has become my signature hat. I first made this hat in the wreath style on a flight to a family vacation at Hilton Head Island, South Carolina. I wanted to create a beautiful floral frame for the face of the baby who would receive it. I remember being thrilled at the way the hat turned out. Later, I transformed the wreath into a bouquet on top of the hat. Both styles look terrific.

Every time I make this hat, it turns out differently. The flowers in this design provide the perfect opportunity to use up leftover yarn from other projects. If you do substitute, be sure to use a DK or light worsted-weight yarn. I have provided a group of colors that look beautiful together, but feel free to try your own combinations. The hat itself can be made in any color as well. I have knitted the hats in Rowan Handknit Cotton in #309 Celery, #310 Shell, and #251 Ecru. These all look great.

skills needed

- Long-tail cast-on (page 20)
- Knit stitch (page 23)
- Knitting in the round on circular needles (page 26)
- Knit 2 stitches together (page 35)
- Knitting in the round on double-pointed needles (page 27)
- Garter stitch (page 32)
- Slip stitch, slip stitch, knit 2 stitches together through the back loops (page 35)
- Sewing on an appliqué (page 41)

size

- Newborn (0–6 months, 6–12 months, 1–2 years, 2 years and up)

yarn

- Rowan Handknit Cotton (100% cotton; 93 yards/50 grams), 1 skein of #252 Black or #263 Bleached
- Tahki Cotton Classic (100% cotton; 108 yards/ 50 grams), 1 skein each (or a small amount) #3003 (ecru), #3459 (dark pink), #3351 (peach), #3549 (gold), #3424 (dark red), #3454 (coral), #3931 (lavender), #3812 (light blue), #3911 (magenta), #3940 (dark purple), #3402 (orange), #3446 (light pink), and #3726 (lime green)

tools

- 16-inch circular needles, U.S. size 7 or size needed to obtain gauge
- Set of 4 double-pointed needles, U.S. size 7 or size needed to obtain gauge
- Set of 2 double-pointed needles, U.S. size 5
- Stitch marker
- Ruler or tape measure
- Scissors
- Yarn needle

gauge

- 5 stitches per inch

HAT

With circular needles and Black or Bleached, use the long-tail method to cast on 56 (64, 72, 80, 88) stitches. Slip a stitch marker onto the right needle to mark the beginning of the round. Join to make a circle for knitting in the round, being careful not to twist the stitches. Knit every round until the hat measures 5 (5½, 6, 6½, 7) inches from the cast-on edge. Next, begin the decrease sequence for the top of the hat.

decrease sequence

Round 1: Knit 6 stitches, knit 2 stitches together. Repeat to the end of the round. 49 (56, 63, 70, 77) stitches remain.

Round 2: Knit 5 stitches, knit 2 stitches together. Repeat to the end of the round. 42 (48, 54, 60, 66) stitches remain.

Round 3: Knit all stitches.

Round 4: Knit directly onto 3 of the size 7 double-pointed needles as follows:

Needle 1: Knit 4 stitches, knit 2 stitches together. Repeat 2 (3, 3, 3, 4) times. 10 (15, 15, 15, 20) stitches are on the first needle.

Needle 2: Knit 4 stitches, knit 2 stitches together. Repeat 2 (3, 3, 3, 4) times. 10 (15, 15, 15, 20) stitches are on the second needle.

Needle 3: Knit 4 stitches, knit 2 stitches together. Repeat 3 (2, 3, 4, 3) times. 15 (10, 15, 20, 15) stitches are on the third needle. 35 (40, 45, 50, 55) total stitches remain.

Use the fourth, or free, double-pointed needle to knit the stitches on each needle for the following rounds.

Round 5: Knit all stitches.

Round 6: Knit 3 stitches, knit 2 stitches together. Repeat to the end of the round. 28 (32, 36, 40, 44) stitches remain.

Rounds 7 and 8: Knit all stitches.

Round 9: Knit 2 stitches, knit 2 stitches together. Repeat to the end of the round. 21 (24, 27, 30, 33) stitches remain.

Round 10: Knit all stitches.

Round 11: Knit 1 stitch, knit 2 stitches together. Repeat to the end of the round. 14 (16, 18, 20, 22) stitches remain.

Round 12: Knit 2 stitches together. Repeat to the end of the round. 7 (8, 9, 10, 11) stitches remain.

Cut the yarn, leaving a 6-inch tail, and thread the tail onto a yarn needle. Pull it through the remaining stitches. Pull tightly to completely close the ring. Weave in the tail on the inside of the hat. Weave in the end at the brim of the hat along the cast-on edge so it is hidden in the roll.

rosebuds

wreath • Make 24 (24, 27, 30, 30) rosebuds to go around the brim of the hat. This number may vary slightly, so check as you knit. For the 2 smallest sizes, make 2 rosebuds in each color. For larger sizes, repeat your favorite colors for the additional rosebuds needed.

bouquet • Make 12 (12, 15, 18, 21) rosebuds for the top of the hat. Make 1 rosebud in each color for the 2 smallest sizes. For larger sizes, repeat your favorite colors for the additional rosebuds needed.

Use the size 5 double-pointed needles as straight needles to knit back and forth. Use the long-tail method to cast on 5 stitches. Knit 22 rows in garter stitch.

Next row: Knit 3 stitches, knit 2 stitches together. 4 stitches remain.

Next row: Slip 1 stitch, slip 1 stitch, knit 2 slipped stitches together through the back loops, knit 2 stitches. 3 stitches remain.
Next row: Knit 3 stitches together. 1 stitch remains.

Cut the yarn, leaving an 8-inch tail, and pull the tail through the last stitch. Roll the knitted fabric from the cast-on end to form a rosebud. Sew the bottom of the rosebud together, pushing the yarn needle through the center to the other side of the rolled strip and being certain to catch every layer. Otherwise, the rosebud can be pulled out from the center. Leave the remaining tail attached and use it to secure the rosebud to the hat.

leaves

wreath • Make 10 (13, 16, 19, 22) leaves to place around the wreath.

bouquet • Make 6 (6, 8, 10, 12) leaves to put around the bouquet edge.

Use size 5 double-pointed needles as straight needles to knit back and forth. With lime green, use the long-tail method to cast on 3 stitches.
Row 1: Knit in the front and back of the first stitch, knit 1 stitch, knit in the front and back of the last stitch. 5 stitches.
Rows 2–4: Knit all stitches.
Row 5: Slip 1 stitch, slip 1 stitch, knit 2 slipped stitches together through the back loops, knit 1 stitch, knit 2 stitches together. 3 stitches remain.
Row 6: Knit 3 stitches together. 1 stitch remains.

Cut the yarn, leaving a 6-inch tail, and pull the tail through the remaining stitch.

placement of wreath on hat

Measure 1½ inches from the bottom of the hat and sew the first rosebud to the hat at this point by stitching around the bottom of the bud. The wreath should rest on the rolled brim, but don't worry about making a straight line with the rosebuds. A little variance will give it a more natural and interesting look. Put the colors in any order. Sew each rosebud to the hat using a yarn needle and the remaining tail. Put the rosebuds close together, attaching the adjoining buds by stitching them together. Pull the end of each tail to the inside of the hat and weave in the end. Next, attach the leaves in the same manner, placing them as you see fit. Place some leaves on the top and bottom of the wreath and coming out at different angles. Pull the ends through to the inside and weave them in.

placement of bouquet on hat

Place and sew the rosebuds onto the top of the hat, starting at the center and working outward until the roses form a small bouquet, using a yarn needle and the remaining tails. Put the rosebuds close together and attach the adjoining buds by stitching them together. Pull the end of the tails to the inside of the hat and weave in the ends. Next, attach the leaves in the same manner, placing them around the outside of the bouquet. Pull the ends through to the inside and weave them in.

little pumpkin

Autumn is my favorite time of year. I love the crisp air and pulling my sweaters out of a cedar chest. But most of all, I love pumpkins. Their color is fantastic and warm, and it brings feelings of falling leaves, taking the kids to a pumpkin farm for Halloween, and Thanksgiving with loved ones. I've called all of my children "little pumpkin" at one time or other. A fall baby or toddler will wear this hat with all the warmth of a delicious pumpkin pie baking in the oven.

skills needed

- Long-tail cast-on (page 20)
- Knit stitch (page 23)
- Knitting in the round on circular needles (page 26)
- Purl stitch (page 25)
- Purl 2 stitches together (page 25)
- Knitting in the round on double-pointed needles (page 27)
- Knitting in the front and back of the same stitch (page 27)
- Knit 2 stitches together (page 35)
- Sewing on an appliqué (page 41)

size

- Newborn (0–6 months, 6–12 months, 1–2 years)

yarn

- RYC Cashsoft DK (57% extrafine merino wool/ 33% microfiber/10% cashmere; 142 yards/ 50 grams), 1 skein #510 Clementine
- Small amount brown (shown in Rowan Handknit Cotton [100% cotton; 93 yards/ 50 grams], #253 Tope)
- Small amount green (shown in Rowan Handknit Cotton [100% cotton; 93 yards/ 50 grams], #219 Gooseberry)

tools

- 16-inch circular needles, U.S. size 7 or size needed to obtain gauge
- Set of 4 double-pointed needles, U.S. size 7 or size needed to obtain gauge
- Stitch marker
- Ruler or tape measure
- Scissors
- Yarn needle

gauge

- 5 stitches per inch

HAT

With circular needles and Clementine, use the long-tail method to cast on 64 (72, 80, 88) stitches. Slip a stitch marker onto the right needle to mark the beginning of thr round. Join to make a circle for knitting in the round, being careful not to twist the stitches. Begin working the stitch pattern as follows.

stitch pattern

Every round: Knit 7 stitches, purl 1 stitch. Repeat to the end of the round.
Follow this stitch pattern until the hat measures 5½ (6, 6½, 7) inches from the cast-on edge. Next, begin the decrease sequence for the top of the hat.

decrease sequence

Round 1: Knit 6 stitches, purl 2 stitches together. Repeat to the end of the round. 56 (63, 70, 77) stitches remain.
Round 2: Knit 5 stitches, purl 2 stitches together. Repeat to the end of the round. 48 (54, 60, 66) stitches remain.
Round 3: Knit 5 stitches, purl 1 stitch. Repeat to the end of the round.
Round 4: Knit directly onto 3 of the double-pointed needles as follows:

Needle 1: Knit 4 stitches, purl 2 stitches together. Repeat 3 (3, 3, 4) times. 15 (15, 15, 20) stitches are on the first needle.
Needle 2: Knit 4 stitches, purl 2 stitches together. Repeat 3 (3, 3, 4) times. 15 (15, 15, 20) stitches are on the second needle.
Needle 3: Knit 4 stitches, purl 2 stitches together. Repeat 2 (3, 4, 3) times. 10 (15, 20, 15) stitches are on the third needle. 40 (45, 50, 55) total stitches remain.

Use the fourth, or free, double-pointed needle to knit the stitches on each needle for the following rounds.
Round 5: Knit 4 stitches, purl 1 stitch. Repeat to the end of the round.
Round 6: Knit 3 stitches, purl 2 stitches together. Repeat to the end of the round. 32 (36, 40, 44) stitches remain.
Rounds 7 and 8: Knit 3 stitches, purl 1 stitch. Repeat to the end of the round.
Round 9: Knit 2 stitches, purl 2 stitches together. Repeat to the end of the round. 24 (27, 30, 33) stitches remain.
Round 10: Knit 2 stitches, purl 1 stitch. Repeat to the end of the round.
Round 11: Knit 1 stitch, purl 2 stitches together. Repeat to the end of the round. 16 (18, 20, 22) stitches remain.
Round 12: Knit 2 stitches together. Repeat to the end of the round. 8 (9, 10, 11) stitches remain. Leave the stitches on the double-pointed needles and continue with the stem.

stem

Switch to Tope.
Round 13: Purl 1 round.
Round 14: Knit 1 round.
Repeat rounds 13 and 14 until the stem measures 1 ½ inches.

Cut the yarn, leaving a 6-inch tail, and thread it onto a yarn needle. Pull the tail through the remaining stitches. Pull tightly to completely close the ring. Weave in the ends on the inside of the hat.

leaf

Use 2 of the double-pointed needles as straight needles to knit back and forth. With Gooseberry, use the long-tail method to cast on 3 stitches.
Row 1: Knit in the front and back of the first stitch, knit 1 stitch, knit in the front and back of the last stitch. 5 stitches.
All even rows: Purl all stitches.
Row 3: Knit in the front and back of the first stitch, knit 3 stitches, knit in the front and back of the last stitch. 7 stitches.
Row 5: Knit in the front and back of the first stitch, knit 5 stitches, knit in the front and back of the last stitch. 9 stitches.
Row 7: Knit in the front and back of the first stitch, knit 7 stitches, knit in the front and back of the last stitch. 11 stitches.
Row 9: Knit 4 stitches, knit 2 stitches together 2 times, knit 3 stitches. 9 stitches remain.
Row 11: Knit 1 stitch, knit 2 stitches together 3 times, knit 2 stitches. 6 stitches remain.
Row 13: Knit 1 stitch, knit 2 stitches together 2 times, knit 1 stitch. 4 stitches remain.
Row 15: Knit 1 stitch, knit 2 stitches together, knit 1 stitch. Do not turn. 3 stitches remain. Pass the 2nd and 3rd stitches over the 1st stitch and off the needle.

Cut the yarn, leaving a 6-inch tail. Pull the tail through the remaining stitch.

making up

Thread the leaf tail onto a yarn needle. Sew the leaf to the base of the stem. Thread the stem tail onto a yarn needle. Weave the tail to the back side of the leaf and tack the leaf to the top of the hat with a couple of stitches. Pull the tail through to the inside of the hat and weave it in.

upside-down daisy

I wanted to create a hat that looked like someone had dropped a big flower face down on a baby's head. The petals are made in a heavier worsted-weight yarn to give them a puffier look. This hat is especially fun to view from above.

HAT

With circular needles and Sugar, use the long-tail method to cast on 56 (64, 72, 80, 88) stitches. Slip a stitch marker onto the right needle to mark the beginning of the round. Join to make a circle for knitting in the round, being careful not to twist the stitches. Knit every round until the hat measures 5 (5½, 6, 6½, 7) inches from the cast-on edge. Next, begin the decrease sequence for the top of the hat.

decrease sequence

Round 1: Knit 6 stitches, knit 2 stitches together. Repeat to the end of the round. 49 (56, 63, 70, 77) stitches remain.

Round 2: Knit 5 stitches, knit 2 stitches together. Repeat to the end of the round. 42 (48, 54, 60, 66) stitches remain.

Round 3: Knit all stitches.

Round 4: Knit directly onto 3 of the double-pointed needles as follows:

Needle 1: Knit 4 stitches, knit 2 stitches together. Repeat 2 (3, 3, 3, 4) times. 10 (15, 15, 15, 20) stitches are on the first needle.

Needle 2: Knit 4 stitches, knit 2 stitches together. Repeat 2 (3, 3, 3, 4) times. 10 (15, 15, 15, 20) stitches are on the second needle.

Needle 3: Knit 4 stitches, knit 2 stitches together. Repeat 3 (2, 3, 4, 3) times. 15 (10, 15, 20, 15) stitches are on the third needle. 35 (40, 45, 50, 55) total stitches remain.

Use the fourth, or free, double-pointed needle to knit the stitches on each needle for the following rounds.

Round 5: Knit all stitches.

Round 6: Knit 3 stitches, knit 2 stitches together. Repeat to the end of the round. 28 (32, 36, 40, 44) stitches remain.

Rounds 7 and 8: Knit all stitches.

Round 9: Knit 2 stitches, knit 2 stitches together. Repeat to the end of the round. 21 (24, 27, 30, 33) stitches remain.

Round 10: Knit all stitches.

Round 11: Knit 1 stitch, knit 2 stitches together. Repeat to the end of the round. 14 (16, 18, 20, 22) stitches remain.

Round 12: Knit 2 stitches together. Repeat to the end of the round. 7 (8, 9, 10, 11) stitches remain.

stem

Switch to Shell and knit for 6 rounds. On the next round, knit 2 stitches together until 4 total stitches remain. Switch to Celery and knit all of the stitches onto 1 double-pointed needle. Work I-cord for 2 inches. Bind off the remaining stitches.

Cut the yarn, leaving a 6-inch tail, and pull the tail through the remaining stitch. Thread it onto a yarn needle, pull it through the center of the I-cord, and secure it on the inside of the hat.

petals (make 6)

With white and 2 double-pointed needles used as straight needles to knit back and forth, use the long-tail method to cast on 3 stitches.

Row 1: Knit in the front and back of the first stitch, knit 1 stitch, knit in the front and back of the last stitch. 5 stitches.

Row 2: Purl in the front and back of the first stitch, purl 3 stitches, purl in the front and back of the last stitch. 7 stitches.

Row 3: Knit all stitches.

Row 4: Purl all stitches.

Rows 5–8: Repeat rows 3 and 4 two times.

Row 9: Slip 1 stitch, slip 1 stitch, knit 2 slipped stitches together through the back loops, knit 3 stitches, knit 2 stitches together. 5 stitches remain.

Row 10: Slip 1 stitch, slip 1 stitch, knit 2 stitches together through the back loops, knit 1 stitch, knit 2 stitches together. 3 stitches remain. Bind off the remaining stitches.

Cut the yarn, leaving an 8-inch tail.

making up

Pin the 6 petals in place on the hat with the cast-on end at the base of the stem on the top of the hat. One at a time, thread each tail onto a yarn needle, sew each petal to the hat, then weave in the ends on the inside of the hat.

felted flower child

Denim is one of my favorite fabrics, and this denim yarn is wonderful to knit with. It gives a clean, crisp look to the stitches. The turned-up brim with a flower is a style of hat that has been around forever, but the oversize felted flower gives it a new twist. The matching mother's pin can be worn on a favorite jean jacket or pinned on a felted bag, handbag, or diaper bag. The flower pin makes a great gift, too.

> note • Before beginning, read this important information on washing and working with Rowan Denim yarn. Rowan Denim yarn is manufactured with excess dye, which washes away over time to create a faded look. This dye can also come off on your hands and needles while knitting. While the dye easily washes off hands with soap and water, it can permanently stain wood or bamboo needles, which can then discolor future projects. Try knitting this yarn with aluminum needles, or designate a pair of wood or bamboo needles for use with denim yarn only. After the completed project is machine washed, there is no further problem with the dye.

skills needed

- Long-tail cast-on (page 20)
- Knit stitch (page 23)
- Knitting in the round on circular needles (page 26)
- Knit 2 stitches together (page 35)
- Purl stitch (page 25)
- Purl 2 stitches together (page 35)
- Knitting in the round on double-pointed needles (page 27)
- Backward-loop cast-on (page 22)
- Sewing on an appliqué (page 41)

size

- 0–6 months (6–12 months, 1–2 years)

yarn

- Rowan Denim (100% cotton; 102 yards/ 50 grams), 1 (2, 2) skeins #231 Tennessee
- Manos del Uruguay (100% wool; 138 yards/ 100 grams), 1 skein each of #40 (gold), #115 (red multi), #49 (coral), #01 (pink), and #35 (green); or use small amounts of feltable (not superwash) wool in 5 different colors

tools

- 16-inch and 29-inch circular needles, U.S. size 6 or size needed to obtain gauge
- 24-inch circular needles, U.S. size 10½
- Set of 4 double-pointed needles, U.S. size 6 or size needed to obtain gauge
- Stitch markers
- Ruler or tape measure
- Scissors
- Yarn needle
- Sewing needle and thread
- Pin back for flower pin

gauge

- 5 stitches per inch

HAT

With the 29-inch size 6 circular needles and Tennessee, use the long-tail method to cast on 312 (344, 378) stitches.

> TIP • As you cast on, place a stitch marker every 50 stitches. This way you won't need to keep recounting your stitches.

Row 1: Working back and forth as if on straight needles, knit 1 stitch, knit 2 stitches together to last stitch, knit 1 stitch. 157 (173, 190) stitches remain.

Row 2: Purl 1 stitch, purl 2 stitches together to last stitch, purl 1 stitch. 80 (88, 96) stitches remain.

Knit the next row onto the 16-inch size 6 circular needles. Slip a stitch marker onto the right needle to mark the beginning of the round. Join to make a circle for knitting in the round, being careful not to twist the stitches.

Rounds 1–10: Knit all stitches.

Round 11: Purl all stitches.

Round 12: Knit 9 (10, 11) stitches, knit 2 stitches together. Repeat to the end of the round. 72 (80, 88) stitches remain.

Knit every round until the hat measures $5\frac{1}{2}$ (6, $6\frac{1}{2}$) inches from the purl row.

Next, begin the decrease sequence for the top of the hat.

decrease sequence

Round 1: Knit 6 stitches, knit 2 stitches together. Repeat to the end of the round. 63 (70, 77) stitches remain.

Round 2: Knit 5 stitches, knit 2 stitches together. Repeat to the end of the round. 54 (60, 66) stitches remain.

Round 3: Knit all stitches.

Round 4: Knit directly onto 3 of the double-pointed needles as follows:

Needle 1: Knit 4 stitches, knit 2 stitches together. Repeat 3 (3, 4) times. 15 (15, 15) stitches are on the first needle.

Needle 2: Knit 4 stitches, knit 2 stitches together. Repeat 3 (3, 4) times. 15 (15, 20) stitches are on the second needle.

Needle 3: Knit 4 stitches, knit 2 stitches together. Repeat 3 (4, 3) times. 15 (20, 15) stitches are on the third needle. 45 (50, 55) total stitches remain.

Use the fourth, or free, double-pointed needle to knit the stitches on each needle for the following rounds.

Round 5: Knit all stitches.

Round 6: Knit 3, knit 2 stitches together.

Repeat to the end of the round. 36 (40, 44) stitches remain.

Rounds 7 and 8: Knit all stitches.

Round 9: Knit 2 stitches, knit 2 stitches together. Repeat to the end of the round. 27 (30, 33) stitches remain.

Round 10: Knit all stitches.

Round 11: Knit 1 stitch, knit 2 stitches together. Repeat to the end of the round. 18 (20, 22) stitches remain.

Round 12: Knit 2 stitches together. Repeat to the end of the round. 9 (10, 11) stitches remain.

Cut the yarn, leaving a 6-inch tail, and thread the tail onto a yarn needle. Pull it through the remaining stitches. Pull tightly to completely close the ring. Weave in the ends on the inside.

felted flower
(make 2 for matching mother's pin)

All of these layers and bobbles are made with Manos del Uruguay wool and size $10\frac{1}{2}$ circular needles. Each layer of the flower is made separately, then stacked from largest to smallest and sewn together before felting.

10-petal flower • With gold and size $10\frac{1}{2}$ needles, use the long-tail method to cast on 112 stitches.

Row 1: Working back and forth as if on straight needles, knit all stitches.

Row 2: Knit 1 stitch. *Knit 1 stitch and pass back to left needle, pass 10 stitches on left needle over this stitch and off the needle, cast on 3 stitches (using the backward-loop method), knit same stitch again. Repeat from * to the last stitch, knit 1 stitch.

Row 3: Knit all stitches.

Cut the yarn, leaving an 8-inch tail, and thread it onto a yarn needle. Pull the tail through all the stitches and join them in a circle. Do not pull tight, so the flower can lay flat. There should be an open circle in the center of the flower.

8-petal flower • With red, cast on 90 stitches. Work rows 1–3 of the 10-petal flower and finish as directed.

Lay this flower inside the 10-petal flower to determine the size of the open circle in the center before securing the circle. The flower should lie inside of, and be slightly smaller than, the previous layer. Do this for each flower layer.

6-petal flower • With coral, cast on 68 stitches. Work rows 1–3 of the 10-petal flower and finish as directed. Check the size of the center circle before securing the circle.

4-petal flower • With pink, cast on 46 stitches. Work rows 1–3 of the 10-petal flower and finish as directed. Pull the inner circle tightly closed and secure the ends.

bobble (make 3)

With green, cast on 1 stitch, leaving a 4-inch tail.
Row 1: Working back and forth as if on straight needles, knit in the front and back of the cast-on stitch until 5 stitches are on the right needle.
Row 2: Knit all stitches.
Row 3: Purl all stitches.
Row 4: Knit all stitches. Do not turn.
Pass the 2nd, 3rd, 4th, 5th stitches over the 1st stitch. Cut the yarn, leaving a 6-inch tail, and thread the tail onto a yarn needle. Stuff the bobble with the 4-inch tail left from casting on, gather up, and secure.

making up flower

With a yarn needle and using the tails, sew the layers together with the 10-petal flower on the bottom and the 8-, 6-, and 4-petal flowers, in that order, on top of it. Securely attach the 3 bobbles to the center of the flower.

felting

Place the flower in a mesh lingerie bag. Pour a small amount of gentle detergent over the bag. Run the flower through a hot wash cycle with a cold rinse. Usually, one washing is enough for this flower. Don't be surprised if your flower comes out of the washing machine in the shape of a ball. Stretch it and form the flower into the desired shape before letting it air-dry. Gently pull and flatten out the layers. Wet wool is very pliable and can be shaped easily.

For the pin, sew the pin back toward the top of the back of the flower with needle and thread.

making up

Sew the separation between the first 2 rows on the ruffle with a yarn needle and the cast-on tail. Weave the end in. Wash the hat in warm water and tumble dry on a gentle cycle. The hat will shrink slightly in length, which has been compensated for in the pattern. Turn up the ruffled edge in the front of the hat. Attach the flower to the hat, slightly off to the side, with a needle and matching thread, and secure the turned-up edge.

TIP • The felted flower will need to be removed before each subsequent washing, as it will continue to shrink in the washing machine. Consider attaching the flower with a strong snap placed toward its top. The snap could secure the ruffle in a turned-up position, as well.

flower pot

I can't seem to get enough of flowers. They're popping up all over this hat and showering out from the top. The basket-weave pattern is easy to do and serves as a perfect guide for placing the crocheted flowers evenly on the base of the hat. The muted colors of the Rowan All Seasons Cotton add subtlety to this hat—so sweet and silly at the same time.

skills needed

- Long-tail cast-on (page 20)
- Knit stitch (page 23)
- Knitting in the round on circular needles (page 26)
- Purl stitch (page 25)
- Knitting in the round on double-pointed needles (page 27)
- Chain stitch (page 42)
- Slip stitch (page 43)
- Single crochet (page 43)
- I-cord (page 39)

size

- Newborn (0–6 months, 6–12 months, 1–2 years, 2 years and up)

yarn

- Rowan All Seasons Cotton (60% cotton/40% microfiber; 98 yards/50 grams), 1 skein each of #202 Soul, #178 Organic, #218 Pansy, #216 Citron, and #217 Lime Leaf

tools

- 16-inch circular needles, U.S. size 7 or size needed to obtain gauge
- Set of 4 double-pointed needles, U.S. size 7 or size needed to obtain gauge
- Stitch marker
- Crochet hook, U.S. size G
- Ruler or tape measure
- Scissors
- Yarn needle

gauge

- 4½ stitches per inch

HAT

With circular needles and Soul, use the long-tail method to cast on 56 (64, 72, 80, 88) stitches. Slip a stitch marker onto the right needle to mark the beginning of the round. Join to make a circle for knitting in the round, being careful not to twist the stitches. Knit until the hat measures 1 inch from the cast-on edge. Next, begin the basket-weave pattern.

basket-weave pattern

Rounds 1–4: Knit 4 stitches, purl 4 stitches. Repeat to the end of the round.

Rounds 5–8: Purl 4 stitches, knit 4 stitches. Repeat to the end of the round.

Repeat rounds 1–8 until the hat measures 5 (5½, 6, 6½, 7) inches from the cast-on edge. Next, begin the decrease sequence for the top of the hat.

decrease sequence

Round 1: Knit 6 stitches, knit 2 stitches together. Repeat to the end of the round. 49 (56, 63, 70, 77) stitches remain.

Round 2: Knit 5 stitches, knit 2 stitches together. Repeat to the end of the round. 42 (48, 54, 60, 66) stitches remain.

Round 3: Knit all stitches.

Round 4: Knit directly onto 3 of the double-pointed needles as follows:

Needle 1: Knit 4 stitches, knit 2 stitches together. Repeat 2 (3, 3, 3, 4) times. 10 (15, 15, 15, 20) stitches are on the needle.

Needle 2: Knit 4 stitches, knit 2 stitches together. Repeat 2 (3, 3, 3, 4) times. 10 (15, 15, 15, 20) stitches are on the needle.

Needle 3: Knit 4 stitches, knit 2 stitches together. Repeat 3 (2, 3, 4, 3) times. 15 (10, 15, 20, 15) stitches are on the needle. 35 (40, 45, 50, 55) total stitches.

Round 5: Knit all stitches.

Round 6: Knit 3 stitches, knit 2 stitches together. Repeat to the end of the round. 28 (32, 36, 40, 44) stitches remain.

Rounds 7 and 8: Knit all stitches.

Round 9: Knit 2 stitches, knit 2 stitches together. Repeat to the end of the round. 21 (24, 27, 30, 33) stitches remain.

Round 10: Knit all stitches.

Round 11: Knit 1 stitch, knit 2 stitches together. Repeat to the end of the round. 14 (16, 18, 20, 22) stitches remain.

Round 12: Knit 2 stitches together. Repeat to the end of the round. 7 (8, 9, 10, 11) stitches remain.

Cut the yarn, leaving a 6-inch tail, and thread the tail onto a yarn needle. Pull it through the remaining stitches. Pull tightly to completely close the ring. Weave in the ends on the inside of the hat.

flower

(make 5 each in Organic, Pansy, Citron, and Lime Leaf, 20 total)

With the crochet hook, chain 4 and join in a ring with a slip stitch.

Round 1: Chain 1 stitch. Work 4 single crochet into the center of the ring. Slip stitch to join the round.

Round 2 (petal round): Work 1 slip stitch into the next stitch, chain 5, slip stitch the same stitch to form petal. Repeat 4 times. Cut the yarn, leaving a 6-inch tail, and pull the tail through the remaining stitch.

i-cord stem

(make 1 each in Organic, Pansy, Citron, and Lime Leaf, 4 total)

With 2 double-pointed needles, use the long-tail method to cast on 3 stitches. Make a 6-inch I-cord. Cut the yarn, leaving a 6-inch tail, and pull the tail through the stitches. Weave in the ends.

making up

Thread the tail of each flower onto a yarn needle and sew 16 flowers (4 in each contrasting color) onto the hat. Sew the flowers onto the purl squares, mixing colors and evenly spacing them on the base of the hat.

Thread the tail of an I-cord onto a yarn needle and attach it to the top of the hat at the center circle. Repeat for the remaining cords. Sew all 4 cords together 1 inch from the hat to stand up and support the flowers. Tie a knot 1½ inches from the end of each cord, pull each cord through the center of a remaining flower, and tie a second knot close to the end to hold the flower in place.

stripes

Stripes are the perfect way to add color to your project but still keep the knitting simple. Carrying colors from row to row is much easier than carrying it along the back from stitch to stitch. I love color and lots of it, and the following techniques allow me to enjoy mindless knitting while working with many colors. I often like to make a more defined break in the stripes by adding a purl row or changing the stitch pattern when starting a new color. It makes the knitting more interesting texturally.

The Marley topper can be added to any simple baby cap and always makes a statement. Don't be fooled by the complex-looking Vertical Stripes pattern; it couldn't be done in an easier way, and it becomes a stitch sampler to show off your beautiful knitting. Add your own stitches to this pattern to create your own panels. You can change the colors to make these hats your own as well.

Any pattern that has stripes or lots of color presents an opportunity to use up leftover yarn from other projects. Check out your stash and see what will work for the new pattern, matching gauge and texture as closely as possible. It feels good to use up your yarn and create something beautiful at the same time.

cotton stria stripes

Manos del Uruguay Cotton Stria is a beautiful textured cotton. The colors are like candy, and knitting with this soft yarn is a complete pleasure. These colorful hats are wonderful when using all of the suggested colors, but you could also use only two or three colors, alternating them.

Note that the hat pattern is given in two color versions. Choose one and purchase the relevant yarns, or come up with your own color combination—perhaps one that combines some Cotton Stria colors used in other hats in this book.

skills needed

- Long-tail cast-on (page 20)
- Knit stitch (page 23)
- Knitting in the round on circular needles (page 26)
- Joining new colors (page 38)
- Purl stitch (page 25)
- Carrying colors (page 38)
- Knit 2 stitches together (page 35)
- Knitting in the round on double-pointed needles (page 27)
- I-cord (page 39)
- Bind off (page 30)

size

- Newborn (0–6 months, 6–12 months, 1–2 years)

yarn

- Choose yarns according to colorway. Manos del Uruguay Cotton Stria (100% cotton; 116 yards/50 grams), 1 skein each of #206 (orange), #203 (olive), #204 (pistachio), #217 (red), #211 (white), #207 (bubble-gum pink), #205 (coral), #201 (grape), #209 (sky blue), #208 (lilac), #210 (aqua), and #213 (mint)

tools

- 16-inch circular needles, U.S. size 6 or size needed to obtain gauge
- Set of 4 double-pointed needles, U.S. size 6 or size needed to obtain gauge
- Stitch marker
- Ruler or tape measure
- Scissors
- Yarn needle

gauge

- 5 stitches per inch

HAT

With bubble-gum pink or aqua and circular needles, use the long-tail method to cast on 64 (72, 80, 88) stitches. Slip a stitch marker onto the right needle to mark the beginning of the round. Join to make a circle for knitting in the round, being careful not to twist the stitches. Knit every round until the hat measures 1 1/2 inches from the cast-on edge. Begin the stripe and stitch pattern and continue this pattern throughout the entire hat.

stripe and stitch pattern

Round 1: Purl all stitches.
Rounds 2–5: Knit every round.
Repeat rounds 1–5, switching to a new color every round 1 as follows:

colorway 1:	colorway 2:
lilac	mint
red	orange
orange	white
white	red
aqua	grape
grape	sky blue
coral	olive
pistachio	aqua
bubble-gum pink	

Continue the stripe and stitch pattern until the hat measures 5½ (6, 6½, 7) inches from the cast-on edge. Next, begin the decrease sequence for the top of the hat and **at the same time** continue the stripe and stitch pattern.

decrease sequence

Round 1: Knit 6 stitches, knit 2 stitches together. Repeat to the end of the round. 56 (63, 70, 77) stitches remain.

Round 2: Knit 5 stitches, knit 2 stitches together. Repeat to the end of the round. 48 (54, 60, 66) stitches remain.

Rounds 3 and 4: Knit all stitches.

Round 5: Knit directly onto 3 of the double-pointed needles as follows:

Needle 1: Knit 4 stitches, knit 2 stitches together. Repeat 3 (3, 3, 4) times. 15 (15, 15, 20) stitches are on the first needle.

Needle 2: Knit 4 stitches, knit 2 stitches together. Repeat 3 (3, 3, 4) times. 15 (15, 15, 20) stitches are on the second needle.

Needle 3: Knit 4 stitches, knit 2 stitches together. Repeat 2 (3, 4, 3) times. 10 (15, 20, 15) stitches are on the third needle. 40 (45, 50, 55) total stitches remain.

Use the fourth, or free, double-pointed needle to knit the stitches on each needle for the following rounds.

Rounds 6–8: Knit all stitches.

Round 9: Knit 3 stitches, knit 2 stitches together. Repeat to the end of the round. 32 (36, 40, 44) stitches remain.

Rounds 10–14: Knit all stitches.

Round 15: Knit 2 stitches, knit 2 stitches together. Repeat to the end of the round. 24 (27, 30, 33) stitches remain.

Rounds 16–20: Knit all stitches.

Round 21: Knit 1 stitch, knit 2 stitches together. Repeat to the end of the round. 16 (18, 20, 22) stitches remain.

Rounds 22–26: Knit all stitches.

Round 27: Knit 2 stitches together. Repeat to the end of the round. 8 (9, 10, 11) stitches remain.

Rounds 28–32: Knit all stitches. Continue in the same color to the end.

Round 33: Knit 2 stitches together to the end of the round. Knit any remaining stitches. 4 (5, 5, 6) stitches remain.

Round 34: *For the newborn size,* go directly to the knotted I-cord.

0–6 month and 6–12 month sizes: Knit 2 stitches together, knit to the end of the round. 4 stitches remain.

1–2 year size: Knit 2 stitches together two times, knit to the end of the round. 4 stitches remain.

knotted i-cord

Put the remaining 4 stitches on 1 double-pointed needle. Make a 2 inch I-cord. Bind off. Cut the yarn, leaving a 6-inch tail, and pull the tail through the remaining stitch. Thread it onto a yarn needle and pull it through the middle of the cord to the inside of the hat. Weave in the end. Tie a knot in the I-cord.

stripey stocking cap

I knitted this hat with blues and greens for my son, Ben, when he needed a new winter hat, and it was quite a hit. What's funny about his hat is that it became a hat *and* a puppet. He would put his hand in the stocking part of the hat to create a mouth and tuck the pom into the mouth. I had to replace the pom at one point due to wear and tear. My two daughters then requested this same hat in different colors. I made Holly's a variety of colors, and Mary Kate's in shades of pink and red and lined it with fleece to eliminate the scratchiness. This hat knits up quickly due to the heavier-weight yarn and the larger-size needles. Create your own colorways to make this hat your child's favorite.

skills needed

- Long-tail cast-on (page 20)
- Knit stitch (page 23)
- Purl stitch (page 25)
- Knitting in the round on circular needles (page 26)
- Seed stitch (page 33)
- Joining new colors (page 38)
- Carrying colors (page 38)
- Knit 2 stitches together (page 35)
- Knitting in the round on double-pointed needles (page 27)
- Purl 2 stitches together (page 35)
- Poms (page 47)
- Whipstitch (page 41)

size

- Newborn (0–6 months, 6–24 months, 2 years and up)

yarn

- Manos del Uruguay (100% wool; 138 yards/ 100 grams), 1 skein each of #66 (red), #101 (dark green multi), #35 (sage), #27 (blue), #40 (gold), and #32 (gray)

tools

- 16-inch circular needles, U.S. size 9 or size needed to obtain gauge
- Set of 4 double-pointed needles, U.S. size 9 or size needed to obtain gauge
- Stitch marker
- Ruler or tape measure
- Scissors
- Yarn needle

optional

- Small amount of fleece for lining (about ⅛ yard)
- Sewing needle and thread

gauge

- 4 stitches per inch

HAT

With red and circular needles, use the long-tail method to cast on 48 (56, 64, 72) stitches. Slip a stitch marker onto the right needle to mark the beginning of the round. Join to make a circle for knitting in the round, being careful not to twist the stitches. Work in seed stitch for 4 rounds. Next, switch to the dark green multi and begin the stitch and color pattern as follows.

stripe and stitch pattern

Rounds 1–6: Knit all stitches.
Switch colors.
Round 7: Purl all stitches.
Repeat rounds 1–7 throughout the entire hat, following this stripe pattern: red, dark green multi, sage, blue, gold, gray.

Continue the stitch and color pattern until the hat measures 4½ (5½, 6, 7) inches from the cast-on edge; end with round 7. If you are at a different round when you reach this measurement, continue round 7. Next, begin the decrease sequence for the top of the hat and **at the same time** continue the stitch and color pattern begining with round 1.

decrease sequence

Round 1: Knit 6 stitches, knit 2 stitches together. Repeat to the end of the round. 42 (49, 56, 63) stitches remain.

Round 2: Knit all stitches.

Round 3: Knit 5 stitches, knit 2 stitches together. Repeat to the end of the round. 36 (42, 48, 54) stitches remain.

Rounds 4–6: Knit all stitches.

Switch colors.

Round 7: Purl directly onto 3 of the double-pointed needles as follows:

Needle 1: Purl 4 stitches, purl 2 stitches together. Repeat 2 (2, 3, 3) times. 10 (10, 15, 15) stitches are on the first needle.

Needle 2: Purl 4 stitches, purl 2 stitches together. Repeat 2 (2, 3, 3) times. 10 (10, 15, 15) stitches are on the second needle.

Needle 3: Purl 4 stitches, purl 2 stitches together. Repeat 2 (3, 2, 3) times. 10 (15, 10, 15) stitches are on the third needle. 30 (35, 40, 45) total stitches remain.

Use the fourth, or free, double-pointed needle to work the stitches on each needle for the following rounds.

Rounds 8–13: Knit all stitches.

Switch colors.

Round 14: Purl all stitches.

Rounds 15–17: Knit all stitches.

Round 18: Knit 3 stitches, knit 2 stitches together. Repeat to the end of the round. 24 (28, 32, 36) stitches remain.

Round 19: Knit all stitches.

Round 20: Knit all stitches.

Switch colors.

Round 21: Purl all stitches.

Rounds 22–27: Knit all stitches.

Switch colors.

Round 28: Purl all stitches.

Round 29: Knit 2 stitches, knit 2 stitches together. Repeat to the end of the round. 18 (21, 24, 27) stitches remain.

Rounds 30–34: Knit all stitches.

Switch colors.

Round 35: Purl all stitches.

Rounds 36–39: Knit all stitches.

Round 40: Knit 1 stitch, knit 2 stitches together. Repeat to the end of the round. 12 (14, 16, 18) stitches remain.

Rounds 41: Knit all stitches.

Switch colors.

Round 42: Purl all stitches.

Rounds 43–48: Knit all stitches.

Switch colors.

Round 49: Purl all stitches.

Round 50: Knit all stitches.

Round 51: Knit 2 stitches together. Repeat to the end of the round. 6 (7, 8, 9) stitches remain.

Rounds 52–55: Knit all stitches.

Switch colors.

Round 56: Purl all stitches.

Rounds 57–61: Knit all stitches.

Cut the yarn, leaving a 6-inch tail, and thread the tail onto a yarn needle. Pull it through the remaining stitches. Pull tightly to completely close the ring. Weave in the tail and any other loose ends on the inside of the hat.

making up

Make a 1-inch pom with 40 wraps. Attach it to the top point of the stocking cap.

optional fleece lining

Cut 3-inch-wide fleece, along the grain so it stretches, long enough to fit inside the rim of the hat with the ends overlapping about ½ inch. Tuck the overlap to the inside and whipstitch with a needle and thread the top and bottom of the fleece and along the joining seam.

rainbow marley

I often look to nature for inspiration. You can't go wrong using color combinations that exist naturally. The rainbow is an example of this. My version is a little brighter than the rainbow in the sky, but the colors look beautiful. This hat is terrific for baby boys or girls, and a perfect alternative to the pale yellow I-don't-know gift that everyone receives before a baby is born. You'll be the hit of the baby shower when you show up with this hat for the mother-to-be.

skills needed

- Long-tail cast-on (page 20)
- Knit stitch (page 23)
- Knitting in the round on circular needles (page 26)
- Joining new colors (page 38)
- Garter stitch (page 32)
- Carrying colors (page 38)
- Purl stitch (page 25)
- Seed stitch (page 33)
- Knit 2 stitches together (page 35)
- Knitting in the round on double-pointed needles (page 27)
- Bind off (page 30)
- Backward-loop cast-on (page 22)

size

- 0–6 months (6–12 months, 1–2 years, 2 years and up)

yarn

- Tahki Cotton Classic (100% cotton; 108 yards/ 50 grams), 1 skein each of #3997 (red), #3402 (orange), #3533 (yellow), #3760 (green), #3808 (blue), #3861 (indigo), and #3940 (violet)

tools

- 16-inch circular needles, U.S. size 7 or size needed to obtain gauge
- Set of 4 double-pointed needles, U.S. size 7 or size needed to obtain gauge
- Stitch marker
- Ruler or tape measure
- Scissors
- Yarn needle

gauge

- 5 stitches per inch

HAT

With red and circular needles, use the long-tail method to cast on 64 (72, 80, 88) stitches. Slip a stitch marker onto the right needle to mark the beginning of the round. Join to make a circle, being careful not to twist the stitches. Knit every round until the hat measures 2 inches from the cast-on edge. Next, begin the stripe and stitch pattern.

stripe and stitch pattern

Rounds 1–4: Work in garter stitch with orange.
Rounds 5–8: Knit all stitches with yellow.
Round 9: Knit with green.
Rounds 10–12: Work in seed stitch with green.
Rounds 13–16: Knit all stitches with blue.
Rounds 17–20: Work in garter stitch with indigo.
Rounds 21–24: Knit all stitches with violet.
Round 25: Knit with red.
Rounds 26–28: Work in seed stitch with red.
Repeat this stripe and stitch pattern until the hat measures 5½ (6, 6½, 7) inches from the cast-on edge.

Begin decrease sequence for the top of the hat and **at the same time** continue stripe and stitch pattern.

decrease sequence

Round 1: Knit 6 stitches, knit 2 stitches together. Repeat to the end of the round. 56 (63, 70, 77) stitches remain.

Round 2: Knit 5 stitches, knit 2 stitches together. Repeat to the end of the round. 48 (54, 60, 66) stitches remain.

Rounds 3 and 4: Knit all stitches.

Round 5: Knit directly onto 3 of the double-pointed needles as follows:

Needle 1: Knit 4 stitches, knit 2 stitches together. Repeat 3 (3, 3, 4) times. 15 (15, 15, 20) stitches are on the first needle.

Needle 2: Knit 4 stitches, knit 2 stitches together. Repeat 3 (3, 3, 4) times. 15 (15, 15, 20) stitches are on the second needle.

Needle 3: Knit 4 stitches, knit 2 stitches together. Repeat 2 (3, 4, 3) times. 10 (15, 20, 15) stitches are on the third needle. 40 (45, 50, 55) total stitches remain.

Use the fourth, or free, double-pointed needle to knit the stitches on each needle for the following rounds.

Rounds 6–8: Knit all stitches.

Round 9: Knit 3 stitches, knit 2 stitches together. Repeat to the end of the round. 32 (36, 40, 44) stitches remain.

Rounds 10 and 11: Knit all stitches.

Round 12: Knit 2 stitches, knit 2 stitches together. Repeat to the end of the round. 24 (27, 30, 33) stitches remain.

Round 13: Knit all stitches.

Round 14: Knit 1 stitch, knit 2 stitches together. Repeat to the end of the round. 16 (18, 20, 22) stitches remain.

Round 15: Knit all stitches.

Round 16: Knit 2 stitches together. Repeat to the end of the round. 8 (9, 10, 11) stitches remain.

Cut the yarn, leaving a 6-inch tail, and thread the tail onto a yarn needle. Pull it through the remaining stitches. Pull tightly to completely close the ring. Weave in the ends on the inside of the hat.

marley topper

(make 1 each in red, yellow, orange, and green)
Use 2 of the double-pointed needles as straight needles to knit back and forth. Use the long-tail method to cast on 18 stitches.

TIP • For the best effect, cast on and bind off tightly.

Row 1: Bind off 17 stitches. 1 stitch remains.

Row 2: Cast on 17 stitches using the backward-loop cast-on method. 18 stitches. Repeat rows 1 and 2 seven times (8 times total). Cut the yarn, leaving a 6-inch tail, and pull it through the remaining stitch.

Take one curly strip and roll it up along the bottom row, with the curls hanging loosely. With a yarn needle and the tail, stitch to secure the roll. Next, wrap the remaining strips one at a time around the first roll and stitch them into place, making one large, curly pom. Sew this to the top of the hat using the remaining ends. Pull all ends through to the inside of the hat and weave them in.

pastel marley

One day I was looking in my basket of leftover Cotton Classic, which is a large collection. I do this often to see if any color combinations strike me as I peer in. This day, I saw these wonderful muted colors come together—colors you may not normally think about combining.

skills needed

- Long-tail cast-on (page 20)
- Knit stitch (page 23)
- Knitting in the round on circular needles (page 26)
- Joining new colors (page 38)
- Garter stitch (page 32)
- Carrying colors (page 38)
- Purl stitch (page 25)
- Seed stitch (page 33)
- Knit 2 stitches together (page 35)
- Knitting in the round on double-pointed needles (page 27)
- Bind off (page 30)
- Backward-loop cast-on (page 22)

size

- Newborn (0–6 months, 6–12 months, 1–2 years)

yarn

- Tahki Cotton Classic (100% cotton; 108 yards/ 50 grams), 1 skein each of #3795 (gray), #3351 (peach), #3701 (lime), #3454 (rose), #3446 (light pink), and #3549 (gold)

tools

- 16-inch circular needles, U.S. size 7 or size needed to obtain gauge
- Set of 4 double-pointed needles, U.S. size 7 or size needed to obtain gauge
- Stitch marker
- Ruler or tape measure
- Scissors
- Yarn needle

gauge

- 5 stitches per inch

HAT

With gray and circular needles, use the long-tail method to cast on 64 (72, 80, 88) stitches. Slip a stitch marker onto the right needle to mark the beginning of the round. Join to make a circle for knitting in the round, being careful not to twist the stitches. Knit until the hat measures 2 inches from the cast-on edge. Begin the stripe and stitch pattern.

stripe and stitch pattern

Rounds 1 and 2: Knit all stitches with peach.
Rounds 3 and 4: Knit all stitches with lime.
Round 5: Knit all stitches with peach.
Rounds 6–9: Work in garter stitch with rose.
Rounds 10–12: Knit all stitches with light pink.
Round 13: Knit 1 stitch light pink, knit 1 stitch gold. Repeat to the end of the round, carrying the colors along the back.
Rounds 14–17: Work in seed stitch with gold.
Round 18: Knit all stitches with gray.
Round 19: Knit all stitches with peach.
Round 20: Knit all stitches with lime.
Round 21: Knit all stitches with peach.
Round 22: Knit all stitches with lime.
Round 23: Knit all stitches with gray.
Rounds 24–27: Work in garter stitch with light pink.
Rounds 28–31: Knit all stitches with rose.
Rounds 32–35: Knit all stitches with gold.
Repeat this pattern until the hat measures 5½ (6, 6½, 7) inches from the cast-on edge. Next, begin the decrease sequence for the top of the hat, continuing in the stripe and stitch pattern.

decrease sequence

Round 1: Knit 6 stitches, knit 2 stitches together. Repeat to the end of the round. 56 (63, 70, 77) stitches remain.

Round 2: Knit 5 stitches, knit 2 stitches together. Repeat to the end of the round. 48 (54, 60, 66) stitches remain.

Rounds 3 and 4: Knit all stitches.

Round 5: Knit onto 3 of the double-pointed needles as follows:

Needle 1: Knit 4 stitches, knit 2 stitches together. Repeat 3 (3, 3, 4) times. 15 (15, 15, 20) stitches are on the first needle.

Needle 2: Knit 4 stitches, knit 2 stitches together. Repeat 3 (3, 3, 4) times. 15 (15, 15, 20) stitches are on the second needle.

Needle 3: Knit 4 stitches, knit 2 stitches together. Repeat 2 (3, 4, 3) times. 10 (15, 20, 15) stitches are on the third needle. 40 (45, 50, 55) total stitches remain.

Use the fourth, or free, double-pointed needle to knit the stitches on each needle for the following rounds.

Rounds 6–8: Knit all stitches.

Round 9: Knit 3 stitches, knit 2 stitches together. Repeat to the end of the round. 32 (36, 40, 44) stitches remain.

Rounds 10 and 11: Knit all stitches.

Round 12: Knit 2 stitches, knit 2 stitches together. Repeat to the end of the round. 24 (27, 30, 33) stitches remain.

Round 13: Knit all stitches.

Round 14: Knit 1 stitch, knit 2 stitches together. Repeat to the end of the round. 16 (18, 20, 22) stitches remain.

Round 15: Knit all stitches.

Round 16: Knit 2 stitches together. Repeat to the end of the round. 8 (9, 10, 11) stitches remain.

Cut the yarn, leaving a 6-inch tail, and thread the tail onto a yarn needle. Pull it through the remaining stitches. Pull tightly to completely close the ring. Weave in the ends on the inside of the hat.

marley topper

(make 1 each in lime, light pink, rose, and peach)

Use 2 of the double-pointed needles as straight needles to knit back and forth. Use the long-tail method to cast on 18 stitches.

TIP • For best effect, cast on and bind off tightly.

Row 1: Bind off 17 stitches. 1 stitch remains.

Row 2: Cast on 17 stitches using the backward-loop method. 18 stitches.

Repeat rows 1 and 2 seven times (8 times total).

Cut the yarn, leaving a 6-inch tail, and pull it through the remaining stitch.

Take one curly strip and roll it up along the bottom row, with the curls hanging loosely. With a yarn needle and the tail, stitch to secure the roll. Next, wrap the remaining strips one at a time around the first roll and stitch them into place, making one large, curly pom. Sew this to the top of the hat using the remaining ends. Pull all the ends through to the inside of the hat and weave them in.

vertical stripes

I wanted to create a vertical-stripe hat pattern using different colors and textures, but I didn't want to carry the colors across the back of the knitting. So to remedy this, I worked out this technique of knitting separate panels and knitting them together as you go. The technique used to attach the panels as you work creates a kind of homespun quiltlike appearance, which I love. The beauty of this hat is that it appears trickier than it is, and there is no seaming at the end. You will get oohs and aahs from everyone with this unusual, textured hat.

skills needed

- Long-tail cast-on (page 20)
- Knit stitch (page 23)
- Knitting in the round on circular needles (page 26)
- Purl stitch (page 25)
- Seed stitch (page 33)
- Bind off (page 30)
- Joining new colors (page 38)
- Garter stitch (page 32)
- Stockinette stitch (page 32)
- Twisted stitch (page 32)
- Basket weave (page 33)
- Cable pattern (page 33)
- Running stitch (page 45)

size

- 0–6 months (6–12 months, 1–2 years, 2 years and up)

yarn

- Rowan Handknit Cotton (100% cotton; 93 yards/ 50 grams), 1 skein each of #320 Buttercup, #263 Bleached, #319 Mango Fool, #303 Sugar, and #318 Seafarer

tools

- 16-inch circular needles, U.S. size 7 or size needed to obtain gauge
- Set of 2 double-pointed needles, U.S. size 7 or size needed to obtain gauge
- Cable needle
- Stitch marker
- Ruler or tape measure
- Scissors
- Yarn needle

gauge

- 5 stitches per inch

HAT

With Seafarer and circular needles, use the long-tail method to cast on 64 (72, 80, 88) stitches. Slip a stitch marker onto the right needle to mark the beginning of the round. Join to make a circle for knitting in the round, being careful not to twist the stitches. Knit every round until the hat measures 1 inch from the cast-on edge.

With Seafarer, switch to knitting back and forth with 2 of the double-pointed needles used as straight needles. Knit 8 stitches onto 1 double-pointed needle, leaving the remaining stitches on the circular needle. Working back and forth on these 8 stitches, work in seed stitch until the strip measures 9 inches from the beginning of the panel. Bind off.

Note • All following panels will be joined to the preceding panel as they are knit, as follows: When knitting on the right side of a panel, with the right needle, pick up a stitch by putting the needle through the first stitch on the left side of the preceding panel, wrapping the yarn around the needle, and pulling through a new stitch. Place this stitch on the left needle and knit or purl the first two stitches together as directed for the panel you are making. This joining stitch is done every other row, right side only, until the panel measures 7 inches from the cast-on edge. Work the panel separately for the remaining 2 inches. Knit every strip this way, picking up a stitch from the last panel and knitting it together with the first stitch of the current panel until the final panel. See page 111 for completing the final panel.

Attach Bleached in position to work the next 8 stitches. With 1 double-pointed needle, knit the next 8 stitches off the circular needle. Working back and forth on these 8 stitches, and joining this panel to the previous panel as you knit, work in garter stitch until the panel measures 7 inches, then work separately until the panel measures 9 inches from the beginning of the panel. Bind off and weave in the end.

Attach Buttercup and, with 1 double-pointed needle, knit the next 8 stitches off the circular needle. Work in stockinette stitch, picking up a stitch from the previous panel and knitting together with first stitch every right-side row until the panel measures 7 inches, then work separately until the panel measures 9 inches from the beginning of the panel. Bind off and weave in the end.

Attach Sugar and work next 8 stitches in twisted stitch as follows:

Row 1: Knit 1 stitch. Knit in second stitch on the left needle and leave it on the needle, knit in the first stitch, and take both stitches off the left needle. Repeat the twisted stitch 2 times. Knit 1 stitch.

Row 2: Purl all stitches.

Repeat rows 1 and 2, joining the panels as you work, until the panel measures 7 inches, then work separately until the panel measures 9 inches from the beginning of the panel. Bind off and weave in the end.

Attach Bleached and work the basket weave pattern over the next 8 stitches as follows:

Row 1: Knit 4 stitches, purl 4 stitches.

Row 2: Knit 4 stitches, purl 4 stitches.

Rows 3 and 4: Repeat rows 1 and 2.

Row 5: Purl 4 stitches, knit 4 stitches.

Row 6: Purl 4 stitches, knit 4 stitches.

Rows 7 and 8: Repeat rows 5 and 6.

Repeat rows 1–8, joining the panels as you work, until the panel measures 7 inches, then work separately until the panel measures 9 inches from the beginning of the panel.

Attach Mango Fool and work the next 8 stitches in cable pattern as follows:

Row 1: Knit all stitches.

Row 2: Purl all stitches.

Row 3 (cable row): Knit 1 stitch, slip the next 3 stitches onto a cable needle and hold it to the front of your work, knit the next 3 stitches, knit 3 stitches from the cable needle, knit 1 stitch.

Row 4: Purl all stitches.

Row 5: Knit all stitches.

Row 6: Purl all stitches.

Row 7: Knit all stitches.

Row 8: Purl all stitches.

Repeat rows 3–8, joining the panels as you work, until the panel measures 7 inches, then work separately until the panel measures 9 inches from the beginning of the panel.

With these 6 panels completed, there are 2 (3, 4, 5) panels left to work. Select which pattern and color you want to repeat for each panel and knit these panels with the stitches that remain on the circular needle.

Note • On the final panel, attach both sides as you work, as follows: On the right-side rows only, join the first stitch as you did the other panels, knit to the last stitch. Pick up a stitch on the right needle by putting the needle through the first stitch on the right side of the first panel, wrapping the yarn around the needle, and pulling through a new stitch. Place this stitch on the left needle, and knit or purl the last two stitches together as directed for the panel you are making. Do this joining stitch on both sides of the final panel until it measures 7 inches from the cast-on edge of the panel. Work the rest of the panel without joining for 2 more inches. On the right side, pick up 1 stitch from the previous panel, work to the last stitch. Work the last stitch together with 1 stitch picked up from the right side of the first panel.

making up

Cut an 8-inch length of Bleached. Thread it onto a yarn needle and attach it to the inside of the hat 7 inches from the beginning of the panel (8 inches from the cast-on edge). Sew running stitch through each panel, pull tight to gather, and close panels, forming the top of the hat. Pull the end to the inside, secure it, and weave it in. Arrange the 2-inch panels at the top.

pink paper bag

This design reminds me of gathering up a brown paper lunch sack at the top and squeezing it together to keep it closed. This hat is much cuter than that old paper bag, but the shape is similar. The picot edge gives a finished detail, and the eyelet round near the top makes stringing the cord a snap.

skills needed
- Long-tail cast-on (page 20)
- Knit stitch (page 23)
- Purl stitch (page 25)
- Seed stitch (page 33)
- Garter stitch (page 32)
- Knitting in the round on circular needles (page 26)
- Yarn over (page 36)
- Knit 2 stitches together (page 35)
- Bind off (page 30)
- Pick up and knit (page 37)
- Backward-loop cast-on (page 22)
- I-cord (page 39)

size
- 0–6 months (6–12 months, 1–2 years, 2 years and up)

yarn
- Classic Elite Provence (100% cotton; 100 yards/ 100 grams), 1 skein each of #2625 Rosa Rugosa, #2689 Bermuda Sand, and #2601 Bleach

tools
- 16-inch circular needles, U.S. size 7 or size needed to obtain gauge
- Set of 2 double-pointed needles, U.S. size 7 or size needed to obtain gauge
- Stitch marker
- Ruler or tape measure
- Scissors
- Yarn needle

gauge
- 5 stitches per inch

HAT

With Rosa Rugosa and circular needles, use the long-tail method to cast on 64 (72, 80, 88) stitches. Slip a stitch marker onto the right needle to mark the beginning of the round. Join to make a circle for knitting in the round, being careful not to twist the stitches. Work in seed stitch until the hat measures 1 inch from the cast-on edge. Next, begin the stripe and stitch pattern.

stripe and stitch pattern

Rounds 1–4: Knit all stitches with Bermuda Sand.

Rounds 5–8: Work in garter stitch with Rosa Rugosa.

Rounds 9–12: Knit all stitches with Bermuda Sand.

Round 13: Knit all stitches with Rosa Rugosa.

Rounds 14–17: Work in seed stitch with Rosa Rugosa.

Rounds 18–21: Knit all stitches with Bermuda Sand.

Rounds 22–25: Work in garter stitch with Rosa Rugosa.

Rounds 26–29: Knit all stitches with Bermuda Sand.

Repeat rounds 13–29 until the hat measures 6 (6½, 6½, 7) inches from the cast-on edge. Switch to Rosa Rugosa.

Next round: Knit all stitches.

Next round: Knit 3 (4, 5, 6), yarn over, knit 2 stitches together, knit 1 stitch, yarn over, knit 2 stitches together. Repeat to the end of the round, creating eyelets for the tie.

Next round: Knit with the same color, knitting through the back loop of yarn overs from the previous round.
Next round: Knit all stitches.
Switch colors and knit one round, then work in seed stitch for 2 inches.

Bind off all stitches. Cut the yarn, leaving a 6-inch tail, and pull the tail through the last stitch. Weave in the ends on the inside of the hat.

picot trim
Using Bleach and circular needles, pick up 64 (72, 80, 88) stitches along the bottom edge of the hat.
Round 1: Knit all stitches.
Round 2: Knit 1 stitch, slip that stitch onto the left needle, cast on 2 stitches with backward-loop method, bind off 4 stitches. Repeat to the end of the round.

Cut the yarn and pull the tail through the remaining stitch. Weave in the end on the inside of the hat. Repeat the picot trim along the top edge of the hat.

i-cord tie
With Bleach and 2 double-pointed needles used as straight needles, cast on 3 stitches and make a 22-inch I-cord to thread through the eyelet holes.

Cut the yarn and pull the tail through the stitches. Tie knots at the ends of the cord. Weave in ends. Weave the I-cord through the eyelet holes. Pull to gather the hat, and tie the cord in a bow.

dots

I can never get enough of dots. I have dotted plates, dotted fabrics in my home, dotted stationery and tissue paper, and I love to knit dots whenever I can. I especially like dotted patterns that are oblong, imperfect, and overlapping. These create interesting, colorful fabrics, and they are wonderful for babies.

The pattern for Dotty is especially simple because the hat is a rectangle folded in half, and the dots are knitted in garter stitch and applied later. This collection also includes some easy embroidery techniques and simple crochet. One of my favorite hats to knit is the Reversible Stripes and Dots. The richness in texture and feel of this hat is dreamy due to the layers of soft cotton denim. You should really give this one a try.

Olive You! is another love of mine. From knock-knock jokes to painted bowls to this hat, my passion for olives is apparent. Plus, I love eating them! I have made Olive You! many times in many forms, and I think it's funny every time.

Dots and babies come in all shapes and sizes. Knit something that's right for your baby, and be sure to include some dots.

dotty

My daughters, Holly and Mary Kate, wore this hat design all through preschool. For them, I lined the inner brim with fleece for extra warmth and comfort. I love using lots of colors, but I don't love carrying lots of colors across the back of my knitting. Dotty is a perfect example of how you can knit a simple one-color hat—and this hat couldn't be any easier—and add color later.

skills needed

- Long-tail cast-on (page 20)
- Knit stitch (page 23)
- Purl stitch (page 25)
- Seed stitch (page 33)
- Bind off (page 30)
- Pick up and knit (page 37)
- Mattress stitch (page 40)
- Knit in the front and back of the same stitch (page 36)
- Slip stitch, slip stitch, knit 2 stitches together through the back loops (page 35)
- Knit 2 stitches together (page 35)
- Tassels (page 48)
- Sewing on an appliqué (page 41)

size

- Newborn (0–6 months, 6–24 months, 2 years and up)

yarn

- Debbie Bliss Merino Aran (100% merino wool; 86 yards/50 grams), 2 skeins #003 (tan), small amounts of #606 (purple), #700 (red), #505 (yellow), #205 (denim), and #701 (navy)

tools

- 24-inch straight or circular needles, U.S. size 7 or size needed to obtain gauge
- Ruler or tape measure
- Pins
- Scissors
- Yarn needle

gauge

- 5 stitches per inch

HAT

With tan, use the long-tail method to cast on 32 (36, 40, 44) stitches. Work back and forth in seed stitch for 6 rows. Change to stockinette stitch (knit 1 row, purl 1 row) and work until the piece measures 11 (11½, 12, 12½) inches from the beginning. Complete 6 more rows in seed stitch. Bind off loosely.

With red, pick up and knit 32 (36, 40, 44) stitches across the cast-on edge. Bind off loosely. Repeat on the bind-off edge.

Fold the piece in half and sew the side seams together using mattress stitch. The seed stitch border forms the edge of the hat opening.

dots

The dots are made separately and sewn on as appliqués. Dots can be placed anywhere on the hat, including the seed stitch border and the side seams. They can also be overlapped. When sewing dots onto the hat, you can stretch them to create different forms or shape them into circles. Pin the dots on before sewing them in place as desired. The sample hat has dots as follows (the 2 smallest sizes won't need as many):

1 small purple dot (to place on red dot)
1 small yellow dot (to place on red dot)
5 small navy dots (one to place on red dot)
4 medium yellow dots
3 medium purple dots
3 large denim dots
3 extra-large red dots

small dot • Cast on 3 stitches. Knit 3 rows. Bind off. Cut the yarn, leaving a 4-inch tail. Form the dot into a circle when sewing it on.

medium dot • Cast on 3 stitches.
Row 1: Knit in the front and back of the first stitch, knit 1 stitch, knit in the front and back of the last stitch. 5 stitches.
Rows 2–4: Knit all stitches.
Row 5: Slip 1 stitch, slip 1 stitch, knit 2 slipped stitches together through the back loops, knit 1 stitch, knit 2 stitches together. 3 stitches remain.
Bind off. Cut the yarn, leaving a 6-inch tail, and pull it through the remaining stitch.

large dot • Cast on 3 stitches.
Row 1: Knit in the front and back of the first stitch, knit 1 stitch, knit in the front and back of the last stitch. 5 stitches.
Row 2: Knit in the front and back of the first stitch, knit 3 stitches, knit in the front and back of the last stitch. 7 stitches.
Rows 3–5: Knit all stitches.
Row 6: Slip 1 stitch, slip 1 stitch, knit 2 slipped stitches together through the back loops, knit 3 stitches, knit 2 stitches together. 5 stitches remain.
Row 7: Slip 1 stitch, slip 1 stitch, knit 2 slipped stitches together through the back loops, knit 1 stitch, knit 2 stitches together. 3 stitches remain.
Bind off. Cut the yarn, leaving a 6-inch tail, and pull it through the remaining stitch.

extra-large dot • Cast on 3 stitches.
Row 1: Knit in the front and back of the first stitch, knit 1 stitch, knit in the front and back of the last stitch. 5 stitches.

Row 2: Knit in the front and back of the first stitch, knit 3 stitches, knit in the front and back of the last stitch. 7 stitches.
Row 3: Knit in the front and back of the first stitch, knit 5 stitches, knit in the front and back of the last stitch. 9 stitches.
Rows 4–6: Knit all stitches.
Row 7: Slip 1 stitch, slip 1 stitch, knit 2 slipped stitches together through the back loops, knit 5 stitches, knit 2 stitches together. 7 stitches remain.
Row 8: Slip 1 stitch, slip 1 stitch, knit 2 slipped stitches together through the back loops, knit 3 stitches, knit 2 stitches together. 5 stitches remain.
Row 9: Slip 1 stitch, slip 1 stitch, knit 2 slipped stitches together through the back loops, knit 1 stitch, knit 2 stitches together. 3 stitches remain.
Bind off. Cut the yarn, leaving a 6-inch tail, and pull it through the remaining stitch.

tassels
Make six 1-inch tassels with 40 wraps. Attach 3 tassels to each corner of the hat. The sample has tassels as follows:
1 red
2 yellow
1 purple
2 denim
Cut a piece of cardboard about 4 inches by 1 inch. Wrap the yarn around the 1-inch width 40 times. Cut an 8-inch piece of yarn and thread it onto a yarn needle. Run the yarn under all strands at the upper end of the cardboard and tie a knot. Pull the tassel off the cardboard. Cut another 8-inch piece of yarn. Tie it tightly around all of the strands toward the top of the tassel and secure with a knot. Cut the loops at the bottom and trim them evenly.

olive you!

This hat was inspired by my family's favorite knock-knock joke. My five-year-old and I still have a sweet giggle over this one. Here it is:

Knock-knock.

Who's there?

Olive.

Olive who?

Olive you!

skills needed

- Long-tail cast-on (page 20)
- Knit stitch (page 23)
- Purl stitch (page 26)
- Seed stitch (page 33)
- Knitting in the round on circular needles (page 26)
- 3-needle bind off (page 31)
- Single crochet (page 43)
- Slip stitch (page 43)
- Knit in the front and back of the same stitch (page 36)
- Purl in the front and back of the same stitch (page 36)
- Slip stitch, slip stitch, knit 2 stitches together through the back loops (page 35)
- Knit 2 stitches together (page 35)
- Purl 2 stitches together (page 35)
- Sewing on an appliqué (page 41)
- Backstitch (page 44)
- Poms (page 47)

size

- Newborn (0–6 months, 6–12 months, 1–2 years, 2 years and up)

yarn

- Rowan Kid Classic (70% lambswool/26% kid mohair/4% nylon; 151 yards/50 grams), 1 skein #828 Feather
- RYC Cashcotton DK (35% cotton/24% polyamide/18% angora/13% viscose/9% cashmere; 142 yards/50 grams), 1 skein #603 Apple
- RYC Cashsoft DK (57% extrafine merino wool/33% microfiber/10% cashmere; 142 yards/50 grams), 1 skein #512 Poppy

tools

- 16-inch circular needles, U.S. size 7 or size needed to obtain gauge
- Set of 2 double-pointed needles, U.S. size 7 or size needed to obtain gauge
- Stitch marker
- Ruler or tape measure
- Scissors
- Pins
- Crochet hook, U.S. size E
- Yarn needle

gauge

- 5 stitches per inch

HAT

With circular needles and Feather, use the long-tail method to cast on 56 (64, 72, 80, 88) stitches. Slip a stitch marker onto the right needle to mark the beginning of the round. Join to make a circle for knitting in the round, being careful not to twist the stitches. Work in seed stitch for 4 rounds. Then, knit every round until the hat measures 4½ (5, 5½, 6, 6½) inches from the cast-on edge. Turn the hat inside out. Use 3-needle bind-off to finish. Turn the hat right side out when finished.

edging

With right side facing and Poppy, single crochet around the bottom edge of the hat, joining the round with a slip stitch. Repeat using Apple.

olive (make 4 for the 2 smaller sizes, 6 for the 3 larger sizes)

Use 2 double-pointed needles as straight needles to knit back and forth. With Apple, cast on 5 stitches.

Row 1: Knit in the front and back of the first stitch, knit 3 stitches, knit in the front and back of the last stitch. 7 stitches.

Row 2: Purl in the front and back of the first stitch, purl 5 stitches, purl in the front and back of the last stitch. 9 stitches.

Row 3: Knit in the front and back of the first stitch, knit 9 stitches, knit in the front and back of the last stitch. 11 stitches.

Row 4: Purl in the front and back of the first stitch, purl 11 stitches, purl in the front and back of the last stitch. 13 stitches.

Row 5: Knit all stitches.

Row 6: Purl all stitches.

Row 7: Slip 1 stitch, slip 1 stitch, knit 2 slipped stitches through the back loops, knit 9 stitches, knit 2 stitches together. 11 stitches remain.

Row 8: Purl 2 stitches together, knit 7 stitches, purl 2 stitches together. 9 stitches remain.

Row 9: Slip 1 stitch, slip 1 stitch, knit 2 slipped stitches together through the back loops, knit 5 stitches, knit 2 stitches together. 7 stitches remain.

Row 10: Purl 2 stitches together, purl 3 stitches, purl 2 stitches together. 5 stitches remain.

Bind off. Cut the yarn, leaving an 8-inch tail, and pull it through the remaining stitch.

pimiento (make 10 for the 2 smaller sizes, 12 for the 3 larger sizes)

Use 2 double-pointed needles as straight needles to knit back and forth. With Poppy, cast on 3 stitches.

Row 1: Knit all stitches.

Row 2: Purl all stitches.

Bind off. Cut the yarn, leaving a 6-inch tail, and pull the tail through the last stitch.

Sew 6 pimientos to the olives.

making up

Pin the olives and the 6 separate pimientos to the hat as desired, with 3 olives and 3 pimientos per side. One at a time, thread the tails onto a yarn needle to sew the olives and pimientos to the hat. With Poppy and backstitch, embroider Olive You! just above the seed stitch border.

poms (make 2)

Holding together 1 strand each of Poppy, Apple, and Feather, make a 1-inch pom with 10 wraps (30 strands total). Cut three 8-inch strands of Poppy. Thread them onto a yarn needle and pull them through the center tie of the pom until the ends meet. Divide these 6 strands into groups of two, braid for 2 inches, and tie a knot. Attach by pulling all of the ends through the top of the hat and tying them off on the inside of the hat.

reversible stripes and dots

This denim hat feels as comforting as an old pair of jeans. I knitted a denim sweater many years ago, and wear and wash it constantly. It just gets better every time. I like the idea of a reversible denim hat, and I wanted each side somehow to be the opposite of the other. I also wanted to be able to see through one side to the other. So I came up with these dots, which are actually holes knitted into the fabric. The wide cuff shows off the alternate side whichever way it is worn. The entire hat just feels good through and through.

skills needed

- Long-tail cast-on (page 20)
- Knit stitch (page 23)
- Knitting in the round on circular needles (page 26)
- Purl stitch (page 25)
- 5 x 3 rib stitch (page 33)
- Joining a new color (page 38)
- Carrying colors (page 38)
- Purl 2 stitches together (page 35)
- Knitting in the round on double-pointed needles (page 27)
- Knit 2 stitches together (page 35)
- Bind off (page 30)
- Backward-loop cast-on (page 22)
- Straight stitch (page 45)
- Single crochet (page 43)

size

- 0–6 months (6–18 months, 18–24 months, 2 years and up)

yarn

- Rowan Denim (100% cotton; 112 yards/50 grams); 1 (1, 2, 2) skeins #324 Ecru, 1 skein each of #231 Tennessee and #229 Memphis

tools

- 16-inch circular needle, U.S. size 6 or size needed to obtain gauge
- Set of 4 double-pointed needles, U.S. size 6 or size needed to obtain gauge
- Stitch marker
- Ruler or tape measure
- Scissors
- Yarn needle
- Crochet hook, U.S. size D

gauge

- 5 stitches per inch

STRIPED HAT

With circular needles and Memphis, use the long-tail method to cast on 64 (72, 80, 88) stitches. Slip a stitch marker onto the right needle to mark the beginning of the round. Join to make a circle for knitting in the round, being careful not to twist the stitches. Begin the ribbed stripe pattern.

ribbing

Every round: Knit 5 stitches, purl 3 stitches. Repeat to the end of the round.

Work in ribbing and stripe pattern **at the same time** as follows:

stripe pattern

4 rounds Memphis
3 rounds Tennessee
2 rounds Memphis
1 round Tennessee
1 round Memphis
1 round Tennessee

Repeat from beginning for stripe pattern. Repeat this ribbed stripe pattern until the hat measures 7½ (8, 8½, 9) inches from the cast-on edge. Next, continuing in stripe pattern, begin the decrease sequence for the top of the hat.

decrease sequence

Round 1: Knit 5 stitches, purl 1 stitch, purl 2 stitches together. Repeat to the end of the round. 56 (63, 70, 77) stitches remain.

Round 2: Knit 5 stitches, purl 2 stitches together. Repeat to the end of the round. 48 (54, 60, 66) stitches remain.

Rounds 3 and 4: Knit 5 stitches, purl 1 stitch. Repeat to the end of the round.

Round 5: Knit onto 3 of the double-pointed needles as follows:

Needle 1: Knit 4 stitches, knit 2 stitches together. Repeat 3 (3, 3, 4) times. 15 (15, 15, 20) stitches are on the first needle.

Needle 2: Knit 4 stitches, knit 2 stitches together. Repeat 3 (3, 3, 4) times. 15 (15, 15, 20) stitches are on the second needle.

Needle 3: Knit 4 stitches, knit 2 stitches together. Repeat 2 (3, 4, 3) times. 10 (15, 20, 15) stitches are on the third needle. 40 (45, 50, 55) total stitches remain.

Use the fourth, or free, double-pointed needle to knit the stitches on each needle for the following rounds.

Rounds 6–8: Knit all stitches.

Round 9: Knit 3 stitches, knit 2 stitches together. Repeat to the end of the round. 32 (36, 40, 44) stitches remain.

Rounds 10 and 11: Knit all stitches.

Round 12: Knit 2 stitches, knit 2 stitches together. Repeat to the end of the round. 24 (27, 30, 33) stitches remain.

Round 13: Knit all stitches.

Round 14: Knit 1 stitch, knit 2 stitches together. Repeat to the end of the round. 16 (18, 20, 22) stitches remain.

Round 15: Knit all stitches.

Round 16: Knit 2 stitches together. Repeat to the end of the round. 8 (9, 10, 11) stitches remain.

Cut the yarn, leaving a 6-inch tail, thread the tail onto a yarn needle, and pull it through the remaining stitches. Pull tightly to completely close the ring. Weave in the ends on the inside of the hat. Machine wash on gentle cycle and tumble dry on low heat. Set aside.

DOTTED HAT

With circular needles and Ecru, use the long-tail method to cast on 64 (72, 80, 88) stitches. Slip a stitch marker onto the right needle to mark the beginning of the round. Join to make a circle for knitting in the round, being careful not to twist the stitches. Begin working as follows:

Rounds 1–4: Knit 5 stitches, purl 3 stitches. Repeat to the end of the round.

Rounds 5–7: Knit all stitches.

Next, begin the dot pattern.

dot pattern

Round 1: Bind off 2 stitches, knit 5 stitches. Repeat to the end of the round.

Round 2: Cast on 2 stitches using the backward-loop method, knit 5 stitches. Repeat to the end of the round.

Rounds 3–9: Knit all stitches.

Round 10: Knit 3 stitches, bind off 2 stitches, knit 2 stitches. Repeat to the end of the round.
Round 11: Knit 3 stitches, cast on 2 stitches using the backward-loop method, knit 2 stitches. Repeat to the end of the round.
Rounds 12–18: Knit all stitches.
Repeat rounds 1–18 of the dot pattern until the hat measures 7½ (8, 8½, 9) inches from the cast-on edge. Next, begin the decrease sequence for the top of the hat.

decrease sequence
Round 1: Knit 6 stitches, knit 2 stitches together. Repeat to the end of the round. 56 (63, 70, 77) stitches remain.
Round 2: Knit 5 stitches, knit 2 stitches together. Repeat to the end of the round. 48 (54, 60, 66) stitches remain.
Rounds 3 and 4: Knit all stitches.
Round 5: Knit onto 3 of the double-pointed needles as follows:
Needle 1: Knit 4 stitches, knit 2 stitches together. Repeat 3 (3, 3, 4) times. 15 (15, 15, 20) stitches are on the first needle.
Needle 2: Knit 4 stitches, knit 2 stitches together. Repeat 3 (3, 3, 4) times. 15 (15, 15, 20) stitches are on the second needle.

Needle 3: Knit 4 stitches, knit 2 stitches together. Repeat 2 (3, 4, 3) times. 10 (15, 20, 15) stitches are on the third needle. 40 (45, 50, 55) total stitches remain.

Use the fourth, or free, double-pointed needle to knit the stitches on each needle for the following rounds.
Rounds 6–8: Knit all stitches.
Round 9: Knit 3 stitches, knit 2 stitches together. Repeat to the end of the round. 32 (36, 40, 44) stitches remain.
Rounds 10 and 11: Knit all stitches.
Round 12: Knit 2 stitches, knit 2 stitches together. Repeat to the end of the round. 24 (27, 30, 33) stitches remain.
Round 13: Knit all stitches.
Round 14: Knit 1 stitch, knit 2 stitches together. Repeat to the end of the round. 16 (18, 20, 22) stitches remain.
Round 15: Knit all stitches.
Round 16: Knit 2 stitches together. Repeat to the end of the round. 8 (9, 10, 11) stitches remain.

Cut the yarn, leaving a 6-inch tail, and thread the tail onto a yarn needle. Pull it through the remaining stitches. Pull tightly to completely close the ring. Weave in the ends on the inside of the hat. Machine wash on gentle cycle and tumble dry on low temperature.

making up
Work straight stitch around each hole on Ecru hat with yarn needle, alternating Memphis and Tennessee for the holes.
Put the wrong sides of the hats together and secure them at the center top with a couple of stitches. Pull one hat inside the other hat with either right side facing out. Hold the bottom edges together. With crochet hook and Tennessee, single crochet the edges together. Crochet loosely to keep elasticity. Turn up the cuff.

medallion

Using only a couple of easy crochet techniques, you can create beautiful accents to add to your knitting. These medallions are fun and simple to make, and they only require three crochet stitches: chain, single crochet, and slip stitch. I made these crochet circles and couldn't wait to use them on a hat. I think the results are terrific!

skills needed

- Long-tail cast-on (page 20)
- Knit stitch (page 23)
- Knitting in the round on circular needles (page 26)
- Knit 2 stitches together (page 35)
- Knitting in the round on double-pointed needles (page 27)
- Chain stitch (page 42)
- Single crochet (page 43)
- Slip stitch (page 43)
- Running stitch (page 45)
- Sewing on an appliqué (page 41)

size

- 0–6 months (6–12 months, 1–2 years, 2 years and up)

yarn

- Hat: Rowan Handknit Cotton (100% cotton; 93 yards/50 grams), 1 skein #309 Celery
- Medallions: RYC Cashcotton DK (35% cotton/ 25% polyamide/18% angora/13% viscose/ 9% cashmere; 142 yards/50 grams), 1 skein each of #604 Geranium, #603 Apple, #605 Magenta, #606 Quartz, #601 Cool

tools

- 16-inch circular needles, U.S. size 7 or size needed to obtain gauge
- Set of 4 double-pointed needles, U.S. size 7 or size needed to obtain gauge
- Pins
- Stitch marker
- Ruler or tape measure
- Scissors
- Yarn needle
- Crochet hook, U.S. size E

gauge

- 5 stitches per inch

HAT

With circular needles and Celery, use the long-tail method to cast on 64 (72, 80, 88) stitches. Slip a stitch marker onto the right needle to mark the beginning of the round. Join to make a circle for knitting in the round, being careful not to twist the stitches. Knit until the hat measures 5½ (6, 6½, 7) inches from the cast-on edge. Next, begin the decrease sequence for the top of the hat.

decrease sequence

Round 1: Knit 6 stitches, knit 2 stitches together. Repeat to the end of the round. 56 (63, 70, 77) stitches remain.

Round 2: Knit 5 stitches, knit 2 stitches together. Repeat to the end of the round. 48 (54, 60, 66) stitches remain.

Round 3: Knit all stitches.

Round 4: Knit directly onto 3 of the double-pointed needles as follows:

Needle 1: Knit 4 stitches, knit 2 stitches together. Repeat 3 (3, 3, 4) times. 15 (15, 15, 20) stitches are on the first needle.

Needle 2: Knit 4 stitches, knit 2 stitches together. Repeat 3 (3, 3, 4) times. 15 (15, 15, 20) stitches are on the second needle.

Needle 3: Knit 4 stitches, knit 2 stitches together. Repeat 2 (3, 4, 3) times. 10 (15, 20, 15) stitches are on the third needle. 40 (45, 50, 55) total stitches remain.

Use the fourth, or free, double-pointed needle to knit the stitches on each needle for the following rounds.

Round 5: Knit all stitches.

Round 6: Knit 3 stitches, knit 2 stitches together. Repeat to the end of the round. 32 (36, 40, 44) stitches remain.

Rounds 7–11: Knit all stitches.

Round 12: Knit 2 stitches, knit 2 stitches together. Repeat to the end of the round. 24 (27, 30, 33) stitches remain.

Round 13–17: Knit all stitches.

Round 18: Knit 1 stitch, knit 2 stitches together. Repeat to the end of the round. 16 (18, 20, 22) stitches remain.

Rounds 19–23: Knit all stitches.

Round 24: Knit 2 stitches together. Repeat to the end of the round. 8 (9, 10, 11) stitches remain.

Cut the yarn, leaving a 6-inch tail, and thread the tail onto a yarn needle. Pull it through the remaining stitches. Pull tightly to completely close the ring. Weave in the ends on the inside of the hat.

medallions

The crocheted medallions are made in the contrasting Cashcotton DK colors. Use all five of the colors, repeating your favorites.

large medallion • (make 6 for the 2 smaller sizes, 7 for the 2 larger sizes)

With one of the Cashcotton DK colors and the crochet hook, chain 4 and join in a ring with a slip stitch.

Round 1: Work 6 single crochet into the center of the ring, join with a slip stitch.

Round 2: Chain 1 stitch. *Work 2 single crochet in the next stitch, 1 single crochet in the following stitch. Repeat from * to the end of the round. Join the round with a slip stitch.

Round 3: Chain 1 stitch. *Work 2 single crochet in the next stitch, 1 single crochet in the following 2 stitches. Repeat from * to the end of the round. Join the round with a slip stitch.

Round 4: Chain 1 stitch. *Work 2 single crochet in the next stitch, 1 single crochet in the following 3 stitches. Repeat from * to the end of the round. Join the round with a slip stitch.

Round 5: Chain 1 stitch. *Work 2 single crochet in the next stitch, 1 single crochet in the following 4 stitches. Repeat from * to the end of the round. Join the round with a slip stitch.

Work one round of picot edging.

small medallion • (make 5 for the 2 smaller sizes, 6 for the 2 larger sizes)

Repeat rounds 1–4 of the large medallion. Work one round of picot edging.

Cut the yarn, leaving a 6-inch tail. Pull it through the remaining stitch.

picot edging

Chain 3 stitches, slip stitch in the same stitch, single crochet in the next stitch, slip stitch in the next stitch. Repeat to the end of the round. Join with a slip stitch.

Cut the yarn, leaving a 6-inch tail. Pull the tail through the remaining stitch.

making up

Attach the large medallions above the brim of the hat by using a running stitch just inside the picot edging. Attach the small medallions the same way, but on the first decrease round of the hat. Attach one large medallion to the top point of the hat as follows: Pinch the center circle together with your fingers to create a flower shape. Sew it together in this shape by running a few stitches through the pinched section of the medallion, then stitch it to the hat. Pull the end through and secure it to the inside of the hat.

sweet treats

Make mine with cherries on top! My vice in life is reflected in the title of this collection of hats. Leave it to me to look at yarn and see cake and candy and anything sweet. These hats are pure fun. With a couple of vintage-inspired bonnets, a wearable birthday cake, a sundae with cherries on top, and a candy-cane mini-stocking cap, there is something for everybody with a sweet tooth here.

Bonnets are simple to make, as they require very little shaping and are knitted back and forth. I added the scarf to the Chocolate Blues bonnet to bring a new dimension to your hat making, plus it looks great and adds warmth. Cherry-O! is a clever little hat—the knitted cherries are worked on double-pointed needles, and the stem is knitted continuously from the top of the cherry. When you're done, all that's left is to attach the cherry stem to the hat. A little crochet and stitch patternwork is added in to sweeten this collection of delicious knitted caps.

birthday cake

I always enjoyed the clothing section at the children's boutique where I helped run a knitting shop. It was filled with cute birthday hats, and I decided to create a knitted version of a hat that celebrates those early birthdays, too. The shop used a large bakery case with cake plates on top to display my hats.

- Long-tail cast-on (page 20)
- Knit stitch (page 23)
- Knitting in the round on circular needles (page 26)
- Purl stitch (page 25)
- Knit 2 stitches together (page 35)
- Knitting in the round on double-pointed needles (page 27)
- Garter stitch (page 32)
- Knit in the front and back of the same stitch (page 36)
- Slip stitch, slip stitch, knit 2 stitches together through the back loop (page 35)
- Slip stitch (page 43)
- Chain stitch (page 42)

size

- 1 year (2 years)

yarns

pink hat

- RYC Cashsoft Baby DK (57% extrafine merino/33% microfiber/10% cashmere; 142 yards/50 grams), 1 skein #800 Snowman
- Tahki Cotton Classic (100% cotton; 108 yards/50 grams), 1 skein #3553 (pink), small amount #3533 (yellow)

blue hat

- RYC Cashcotton DK (35% cotton/ 25% polyamide/18% angora/13% viscose/ 9% cashmere; 142 yards/50 grams), 1 skein each of #600 White and #601 Cool
- Tahki Cotton Classic, small amount #3533 (yellow)

tools

- 16-inch circular needles, U.S. size 7 or size needed to obtain gauge
- Set of 4 double-pointed needles, U.S. size 7 or size needed to obtain gauge
- Set of 2 double-pointed needles, U.S. size 5
- Stitch marker
- Ruler or tape measure
- Scissors
- Yarn needle
- Small amount of polyfill stuffing
- Crochet hook, U.S. size G

gauge

- 5 stitches per inch

HAT

With Snowman and circular needles, use the long-tail method to cast on 80 (88) stitches. Slip a stitch marker onto the right needle to mark the beginning of the round. Join to make a circle for knitting in the round, being careful not to twist the stitches. Knit every round until hat measures 2 inches from the cast-on edge.
Round 1: Purl all stitches.
Rounds 2–5: Knit all stitches.
Round 6: Purl all stitches.
Repeat rounds 1–5 until the hat measures 6 (7) inches from the cast-on edge. Next, begin the decrease sequence for the top of the hat.

decrease sequence
Round 1: Knit 6 stitches, knit 2 stitches together. Repeat to the end of the round. 70 (77) stitches remain.
Rounds 2 and 3: Knit all stitches.

Round 4: Knit 5 stitches, knit 2 stitches together. Repeat to the end of the round. 60 (66) stitches remain.

Rounds 5 and 6: Knit all stitches.

Round 7: Knit directly onto 3 of the double-pointed needles as follows:

Needle 1: Knit 4 stitches, knit 2 stitches together. Repeat 3 (4) times. 15 (20) stitches are on the first needle.

Needle 2: Knit 4 stitches, knit 2 stitches together. Repeat 3 (4) times. 15 (20) stitches are on the second needle.

Needle 3: Knit 4 stitches, knit 2 stitches together. Repeat 4 (3) times. 20 (15) stitches are on the third needle. 50 (55) total stitches remain.

Use the fourth, or free, double-pointed needle to knit the stitches on each needle for the following rounds.

Rounds 8 and 9: Knit all stitches.

Round 10: Knit 3 stitches, knit 2 stitches together. Repeat to the end of the round. 40 (44) stitches remain.

Round 11: Knit 2 stitches, knit 2 stitches together. Repeat to the end of the round. 30 (33) stitches remain.

Round 12: Knit 1 stitch, knit 2 stitches together. Repeat to the end of the round. 20 (22) stitches remain.

Round 13: Knit 2 stitches together to the end of the round. 10 (11) stitches remain.

Cut the yarn, leaving a 6-inch tail, and thread the tail onto a yarn needle. Pull it through the remaining stitches. Pull tightly to completely close the ring. Weave in the ends on the inside of the hat.

candle (make 1)

Use two size 5 double-pointed needles as straight needles to knit back and forth. With pink or blue, use the long-tail method to cast on 8 stitches.

Work garter stitch for 2 inches. Bind off. Using a yarn needle, sew a seam along the side and the top. Stuff the candle with polyfill until firm. Sew it to the top of the hat at the center circle.

flame

Use two size 5 double-pointed needles as straight needles to knit back and forth. With yellow, use the long-tail method to cast on 5 stitches.

Row 1: Knit all stitches.

Row 2: Knit in the front and back of the first stitch, knit 3 stitches, knit in the front and back of the last stitch. 7 stitches.

Rows 3 and 4: Knit all stitches.

Row 5: Slip 1 stitch, slip 1 stitch, knit 2 slipped stitches together through the back loops, knit 3 stitches, knit 2 stitches together. 5 stitches remain.

Row 6: Slip 1 stitch, slip 1 stitch, knit 2 slipped stitches together through the back loops, knit 1 stitch, knit 2 stitches together. 3 stitches remain.

Row 7: Knit 2 stitches together, knit 1 stitch, pull the first stitch over the second stitch and off the needle. 1 stitch remains.

Cut the yarn, leaving an 8-inch tail. Pull the tail through the remaining stitch. Sew the side seam and stuff the flame with extra yellow yarn from the tail. Sew the flame to the top of the candle.

frosting loops

With the crochet hook and pink or blue, and starting at the lowest purl round on the hat, slip stitch through a purl stitch at any starting point. Use the purl rounds as the foundation rounds for the frosting loops. Work as follows:

Chain 6, slip stitch on the 4th purl stitch. Repeat to the end of the round.

Repeat frosting loop round on each of the purl rows. Weave in the ends on the inside of the hat.

candy cane

With its long stocking-cap point, this hat reminds me of an elf hat or a candy cane, but it could certainly be worn at any time of year. Simply adding rows between your decrease rows makes it easy to change the shape of a hat. I kept the pom spindly so as not to weigh down the point of the hat.

skills needed

- Long tail cast-on (page 20)
- Knit stitch (page 23)
- Knitting in the round on circular needles (page 26)
- Knit 2 stitches together (page 35)
- Knitting in the round on double-pointed needles (page 27)
- Joining a new color (page 38)
- Carrying colors (page 38)
- I-cord (page 39)
- Poms (page 47)

size

- Newborn (0–6 months, 6–12 months, 1–2 years, 2 years and up)

yarn

- Rowan Handknit Cotton (100% cotton; 93 yards/50 grams), 1 skein each of #215 Rosso and #251 Ecru

tools

- 16-inch circular needles, U.S. size 7 or size needed to obtain gauge
- Set of 4 double-pointed needles, U.S. size 7 or size needed to obtain gauge
- Stitch marker
- Ruler or tape measure
- Scissors
- Yarn needle

gauge

- 5 stitches per inch

HAT

With circular needles and Rosso, use the long-tail method to cast on 56 (64, 72, 80, 88) stitches. Slip a stitch marker onto the right needle to mark the beginning of the round. Join to make a circle for knitting in the round, being careful not to twist the stitches. Knit 2 rounds in Rosso, then begin stripe pattern.

stripe pattern

Rounds 1 and 2: Knit all stitches with Ecru.
Rounds 3 and 4: Knit all stitches with Rosso.
Repeat rounds 1–4 until the hat measures 5 (5½, 5½, 6½, 7) inches from the cast-on edge. Next, begin the decrease sequence for the top of the hat and **at the same time** continue the stripe pattern.

decrease sequence

Round 1: Knit 6 stitches, knit 2 stitches together. Repeat to the end of the round. 49 (56, 63, 70, 77) stitches remain.
Round 2: Knit 5 stitches, knit 2 stitches together. Repeat to the end of the round. 42 (48, 54, 60, 66) stitches remain.
Round 3: Knit all stitches.
Round 4: Knit directly onto 3 of the double-pointed needles as follows:
Needle 1: Knit 4 stitches, knit 2 stitches together. Repeat 2 (3, 3, 3, 4) times. 10 (15, 15, 15, 20) stitches are on the first needle.
Needle 2: Knit 4 stitches, knit 2 stitches together. Repeat 2 (3, 3, 3, 4) times. 10 (15, 15, 15, 20) stitches are on the second needle.

Needle 3: Knit 4 stitches, knit 2 stitches together. Repeat 3 (2, 3, 4, 3) times. 15 (10, 15, 20, 15) stitches are on the third needle. 35 (40, 45, 50, 55) total stitches remain.

Use the fourth, or free, double-pointed needle to knit the stitches on each needle for the following rounds.

Round 5: Knit all stitches.

Round 6: Knit 3 stitches, knit 2 stitches together. Repeat to the end of the round. 28 (32, 36, 40, 44) stitches remain.

Rounds 7 and 8: Knit all stitches.

Round 9: Knit 2 stitches, knit 2 stitches together. Repeat to the end of the round. 21 (24, 27, 30, 33) stitches remain.

Rounds 10–19: Knit all stitches.

Round 20: Knit 1 stitch, knit 2 stitches together. Repeat to the end of the round. 14 (16, 18, 20, 22) stitches remain.

Rounds 21–30: Knit all stitches.

Round 31: Knit 2 stitches together. Repeat to the end of the round. 7 (8, 9, 10, 11) stitches remain.

Rounds 32–41: Knit all stitches.

With Rosso, knit the remaining stitches onto one double-pointed needle. Begin working I-cord, knitting 2 stitches together across the first row. 4 (4, 5, 5, 6) stitches remain.

On the next row, and continuing in I-cord, knit 2 stitches together 1 (1, 2, 2, 3) times. 3 stitches remain for all sizes.

Continue in I-cord on these 3 stitches for 1 inch. Bind off.

Cut the yarn, leaving a 6-inch tail, and thread the tail onto a yarn needle. Pull it through the remaining stitch. Pull tightly and secure the tail on the inside of the hat.

pom
With Ecru, make a 1-inch pom with 20 wraps. Attach it to the top point of the hat.

chocolate blues

I get a kick out of the names some yarn companies give to the colors of their yarns. The names can inspire a feeling or sometimes even a design, or they can simply make you smile. Rowan is especially clever when it comes to names: The brown Cashsoft is named Donkey and the blue Cashcotton is named Cool. The names caught my attention, and when I saw the combination, I knew they had to be knit together. This vintage-inspired combined scarf and hat is a winner in every category, and the kids will love the poms.

skills needed

- Long-tail cast-on (page 20)
- Knit stitch (page 23)
- Purl stitch (page 25)
- Garter stitch (page 32)
- Stockinette stitch (page 32)
- Joining a new color (page 38)
- Carrying colors (page 38)
- Bind off (page 30)
- Mattress stitch (page 40)
- Whipstitch (page 41)
- Poms (page 47)

size

- 0–6 months (6–12 months, 1–2 years, 2 years and up)

yarn

- RYC Cashsoft DK (57% extrafine merino wool/ 33% microfiber/10% cashmere; 142 yards/ 50 grams), 1 skein #517 Donkey
- RYC Cashcotton DK (35% cotton/25% polyamide/18% angora/13% viscose/9% cashmere; 142 yards/50 grams), 1 skein #601 Cool

tools

- Straight or 24-inch circular needles, U.S. size 7 or size needed to obtain gauge
- Ruler or tape measure
- Crochet hook, U.S. size F
- Scissors
- Yarn needle

gauge

- 5 stitches per inch

BONNET

With Donkey and using the long-tail method, cast on 57 (63, 69, 75) stitches. Work in garter stitch for 4 rows.

Start stripe pattern as follows, working in stockinette stitch:

Row 1: Knit all stitches with Cool.

Row 2: Purl all stitches with Cool.

Row 3: Knit all stitches with Donkey.

Row 4: Purl all stitches with Donkey.

Repeat rows 1–4 for a stripe pattern, carrying colors up the side, until the hat measures 4 (4½, 5½, 6½) inches from the cast-on edge.

Next row: Bind off 23 (24, 25, 26) stitches, knit 11 (15, 19, 20) stitches, bind off 23 (24, 25, 26) stitches.

Cut the yarn, leaving an 8-inch tail. Pull the tail through the remaining stitch.

Reattach the yarn and continue working the stitches in stripe pattern for a further 4 (4½, 5, 5½) inches from the bind-off edge.

Bind off the remaining stitches. The bonnet will form a T shape. With a yarn needle, sew the back flap to the sides using mattress stitch to form the bonnet. Set aside.

SCARF

With Cool and using the long-tail method, cast on 160 stitches. Work in garter stitch for 4 rows. Switch to Donkey and continue as follows:

Row 1: Knit all stitches.

Row 2: Knit 4 stitches, purl to last 4 stitches, knit 4 stitches.

Repeat rows 1 and 2 four times. 10 rows total.

Knit 4 rows.

Bind off.

making up

Fold the scarf in half with the purl side out. Use whipstitch to sew around the edges of the scarf. Find the middle of the scarf and the middle of the back of the bonnet and pin together. Sew the scarf to the bottom edge of the bonnet using whipstitch.

Make 8 poms each in Donkey and Cool, 1 inch in length and 40 wraps. Attach 10 poms evenly spaced around the brim of the bonnet. Attach 3 to each end of the scarf.

marshmallow bonnet

RYC Cashsoft Baby DK has a wonderful feel to it, and the white color reminds me of a fluffy marshmallow. I added Kidsilk Haze, a mohair and silk blend, to soften the fabric even more. It has a vintage feel, and the crocheted accents make it fun. The seed stitch adds a sweet and feminine texture. Once you get the seed stitch down, this is an easy knit because there's no shaping along the way. A turning row—a row that marks the turning under of a hem or brim of a hat—is used to add a picot detail to surround the face of the child. The bobble and crochet loops are optional.

skills needed

- Long-tail cast-on (page 20)
- Knit stitch (page 23)
- Purl stitch (page 25)
- Seed stitch (page 33)
- Yarn over (page 36)
- Knit 2 stitches together (page 35)
- Bind off (page 30)
- Mattress stitch (page 40)
- Pick up and knit (page 37)
- Reverse stockinette stitch (page 32)
- Slip knot (page 42)
- Knit in the front and back of the same stitch (page 36)
- Chain stitch (page 42)
- Slip stitch (page 43)

size

- 0–6 months (6–12 months, 1–2 years, 2 years and up)

yarn

- RYC Cashsoft Baby DK (57% extrafine merino/ 33% microfiber/10% cashmere; 142 yards/ 50 grams), 1 skein each of #800 Snowman and #807 Pixie

optional

(The gauge remains the same with or without)

- Rowan Kidsilk Haze (70% kid mohair/30% silk; 231 yards/25 grams), 1 skein each of #590 Pearl and #580 Grace

tools

- 24-inch circular or straight needles, U.S. size 7 or size needed to obtain gauge
- Ruler or tape measure
- Scissors
- Yarn needle
- Crochet hook, U.S. size F

gauge

- 5 stitches per inch

BONNET

With Snowman and Pearl held together, use the long-tail method to cast on 57 (63, 69, 75) stitches. Work in seed stitch until the hat measures 1 inch from the cast-on edge. Next, work the turning row as follows:

Turning row: Knit 1, yarn over, knit 2 stitches together. Repeat to the last stitch, knit 1 stitch. Continue in seed stitch until the hat measures 4 (4½ , 5½ , 6½) inches from the turning row.

Bind off 23 (24, 25, 26) stitches, knit 11 (15, 19, 20) stitches, bind off 23 (24, 25, 26) stitches.

Cut the yarn, leaving an 8-inch tail. Pull the tail through the remaining stitch.

Reattach the yarn and continue working the rows in seed stitch for a further 4 (4½, 5, 5½) inches from the bind-off edge.

Bind off the remaining stitches. The bonnet will form a T shape. Sew the back flap to the sides using mattress stitch to form the bonnet.

bottom edging

Fold 1 inch toward the inside of the hat at the turning row. As you pick up stitches along the front bottom edge, put the needle through both layers of the hat and the brim to secure.

With right side facing, starting at left front edge and with Snowman and Pearl held together, pick up and knit as follows:
Along left edge, pick up 18 (20, 22, 24) stitches, along back edge pick up 13 (15, 17, 19) stitches, and along right edge pick up 18 (20, 22, 24) stitches. 49 (55, 61, 67) stitches total. Continue in reverse stockinette stitch as follows:

Row 1 (wrong side facing): Knit all stitches.
Row 2 (right side facing): Purl all stitches.
Rows 3 and 4: Repeat rows 1 and 2 one time.

Bind off loosely. Leave the remaining stitch on the needle. Do not cut the yarn.

chin strap

Turn and pick up 2 stitches along the front edge. With 3 stitches on the needle, work in seed stitch for 3 (3½, 3½, 3½) inches.
Next row: Knit 1 stitch, yarn over, knit 2 stitches together.
Next row: Work in seed stitch across the row. Bind off. Cut the yarn, leaving a 6-inch tail, and thread it onto a yarn needle. Pull it through the remaining stitch. Weave in the end.

bobble

With Pixie and Grace held together, make a loose slip knot, leaving a 3-inch tail.
Row 1: Knit in the front and back of the slip knot until 5 stitches are on the right needle.
Row 2: Knit all stitches.
Row 3: Purl all stitches.
Row 4: Knit all stitches. Do not turn. Pass the 2nd, 3rd, and 4th stitches over the 1st stitch.

Cut the yarn, leaving a 6-inch tail. Thread the tail onto a yarn needle and stuff the bobble with the 3-inch tail from the cast-on. Gather up to close, and sew the bobble to the bottom front edge to be used as a button for the chin strap.

crochet loops

With a crochet hook and Pixie and Grace held together, pick up 1 stitch at the top corner of either seam. Chain 10, then slip stitch into the corner. Repeat 12 times. After 12 loops are made, cut the yarn. Pull the tail through to the wrong side and weave it in. Repeat at the other corner.

cherry-o!

When I first made this hat, I used black, cream, and bright red. It was pretty but seemed slightly serious. Using pink and red completely transformed this hat. It was remarkable to me that a simple color change could make such a huge difference. The new colors really make this hat worthy of its fun design.

skills needed

- Long-tail cast-on (page 20)
- Knit stitch (page 23)
- Knitting in the round on circular needles (page 26)
- Joining a new color (page 38)
- Carrying colors (page 38)
- Knit 2 stitches together (page 35)
- Knitting in the round on double-pointed needles (page 27)
- Knit in the front and back of the same stitch (page 36)
- Slip stitch, slip stitch, knit 2 stitches together through the back loops (page 35)
- I-cord (page 39)
- Sewing on an appliqué (page 41)

size

- Newborn (0–6 months, 6–12 months, 1–2 years, 2 years and up)

yarn

- Rowan Handknit Cotton (100% cotton; 93 yards/ 50 grams), 1 skein each of #310 Shell and #215 Rosso, small amount of #219 Gooseberry

tools

- 16-inch circular needles, U.S. size 7 or size needed to obtain gauge
- Set of 4 double-pointed needles, U.S. size 7 or size needed to obtain gauge
- Stitch marker
- Ruler or tape measure
- Scissors
- Yarn needle
- Small amount of polyfill

gauge

- 5 stitches per inch

HAT

With Shell and circular needles, use the long-tail method to cast on 56 (64, 72, 80, 88) stitches. Slip a stitch marker onto the right needle to mark the beginning of the round. Join to make a circle for knitting in the round, being careful not to twist the stitches. Knit until the hat measures 2 inches from the cast-on edge. Next, begin the stripe pattern.

stripe pattern

Rounds 1–4: Knit all stitches with Rosso.
Rounds 5–8: Knit all stitches with Shell.
Repeat stripe pattern until the hat measures 5 (5½, 6, 6½, 7) inches from the cast-on edge. Continuing in Shell only, begin the decrease sequence for the top of the hat.

decrease sequence

Round 1: Knit 6 stitches, knit 2 stitches together. Repeat to the end of the round. 49 (56, 63, 70, 77) stitches remain.
Round 2: Knit 5 stitches, knit 2 stitches together. Repeat to the end of the round. 42 (48, 54, 60, 66) stitches remain.
Round 3: Knit all stitches.
Round 4: Knit directly onto 3 double-pointed needles as follows:
Needle 1: Knit 4 stitches, knit 2 stitches together. Repeat 2 (3, 3, 3, 4) times. 10 (15, 15, 15, 20) stitches are on the first needle.
Needle 2: Knit 4 stitches, knit 2 stitches together. Repeat 2 (3, 3, 3, 4) times. 10 (15, 15, 15, 20) stitches are on the second needle.
Needle 3: Knit 4 stitches, knit 2 stitches together. Repeat 3 (2, 3, 4, 3) times. 15 (10, 15, 20, 15) stitches are on the third needle. 35 (40, 45, 50, 55) total stitches remain.

Use the fourth, or free, double-pointed needle to knit the stitches on each needle for the following rounds.

Round 5: Knit all stitches.

Round 6: Knit 3 stitches, knit 2 stitches together. Repeat to the end of the round. 28 (32, 36, 40, 44) stitches remain.

Rounds 7 and 8: Knit all stitches.

Round 9: Knit 2 stitches, knit 2 stitches together. Repeat to the end of the round. 21 (24, 27, 30, 33) stitches remain.

Round 10: Knit all stitches.

Round 11: Knit 1 stitch, knit 2 stitches together. Repeat to the end of the round. 14 (16, 18, 20, 22) stitches remain.

Round 12: Knit 2 stitches together. Repeat to the end of the round. 7 (8, 9, 10, 11) stitches remain.

With Rosso knit for 1 inch to make stem.

Cut the yarn, leaving a 6-inch tail, and thread it onto a yarn needle. Pull it tightly through the remaining stitches to completely close the ring. Weave in the ends on the inside of the hat.

cherries (make 2)

Using Rosso cast on 9 stitches onto 1 of the double-pointed needles. slip 3 stitches onto each of 2 other double-pointed needlles (3 stitches per needle). Join in a round, being careful not to twist the stitches. Place a marker at the beginning of the round and knit 2 rounds.

increase rounds

Round 1: Knit in the front and back of the same stitch in the first stitch, knit 1 stitch, knit in the front and back of the last stitch on each double-pointed needle. 15 stitches.

Round 2: Knit all stitches.

Round 3: Knit in the front and back of the same stitch in the first stitch, knit 1 stitch, knit in the front and back of the last stitch on each double-pointed needle. 21 stitches.

Rounds 4–6: Knit all stitches.

decrease rounds

Round 7: Slip 1 stitch, slip 1 stitch, knit 2 slipped stitches together through the back loops, knit to last 2 stitches, knit 2 stitches together. Repeat on each double-pointed needle. 15 stitches remain.

Round 8: Knit all stitches.

Round 9: Slip, slip, knit 2 slipped stitches together through the back loops, knit to last 2 stitches, knit 2 stitches together. Repeat on each double-pointed needle. 9 stitches remain.

Rounds 10–12: Knit all stitches.

With polyfill, stuff the cherry while it is still on the double-pointed needles. Thread a yarn needle with the tail from the cast-on edge and sew the bottom of the cherry closed. Weave in the end to the inside of the cherry.

With Gooseberry, and knitting onto 1 double-pointed needle only, knit 1 stitch, then knit 2 stitches together 4 times. 5 stitches remain. Do not turn. Begin I-cord by knitting 2 stitches together on the first row. 4 stitches remain. Work a 4-stitch I-cord for 2 inches. Bind off. Cut the yarn, leaving a 6-inch tail, and thread it onto a yarn needle. Sew the I-cord to the top of the hat at the base of the stem.

leaf

Use 2 of the double-pointed needles as straight needles to knit back and forth. With Gooseberry, use the long-tail method, to cast on 3 stitches.

All even rows: Purl all stitches.

Row 1: Knit in the front and back of the first stitch, knit 1 stitch, knit in the front and back of the last stitch. 5 stitches.

Row 3: Knit in the front and back of the first stitch, knit 3 stitches, knit in the front and back of the last stitch. 7 stitches.

Row 5: Knit in the front and back of the first stitch, knit 5 stitches, knit in the front and back of the last stitch. 9 stitches.

Row 7: Knit in the front and back of the first stitch, knit 7 stitches, knit in the front and back of the last stitch. 11 stitches.

Row 9: Knit 4 stitches, knit 2 stitches together 2 times, knit 3 stitches. 9 stitches remain.

Row 11: Knit 1 stitch, knit 2 stitches together 3 times, knit 2 stitches. 6 stitches remain.

Row 13: Knit 1 stitch, knit 2 stitches together 2 times, knit 1 stitch. 4 stitches remain.

Row 15: Knit 1 stitch, knit 2 stitches together, knit 1 stitch. 3 stitches remain. Do not turn.

Pass the 2nd and 3rd stitches over the 1st stitch.

Cut the yarn, leaving a 6-inch tail. Pull the tail through the remaining stitch. Attach the leaf to the top of the hat at the base of the stem.

embellished hats

Embellishing has become the heart of my designs, although initially I didn't set out for this to happen. It sort of evolved. I was presented with design challenges and had to come up with ways to achieve certain looks with my knitting. I love the idea of making things beautiful and special, but keeping them simple as well. I often study vintage knits, then give them a modern twist. Embellishing is a great way to do this, as it adds a playful dimension to knitting. I keep a running list at the back of my sketch book of new ideas for future designs. Embellishing is fun and can take your knitting to a whole new level.

Embellishing means adding something onto a knitted item after the base is completed. This may be beautiful silk ribbons, knitted appliqués, or embroidery. This embellished collection offers projects for a wide range of skill levels. If you are a beginner, give the patterns a quick read-through before you start, and then look up any skills you're unsure of. Don't be afraid to try something new to stretch your skill level. You will be pleasantly surprised with what you can accomplish with only knit and purl stitches.

sailboat

The sailboat is an old, classic baby motif. It can be the perfect gift for any sea-loving baby. My sister gave this hat to a friend's baby boy. He loved the hat so much that it became his take-everywhere blankie. The pointed shape and the textured appliqué boat give this old favorite a fresh new look.

HAT

With circular needles and denim, use the long-tail method to cast on 64 (72, 80, 88) stitches. Slip a stitch marker onto the right needle to mark the beginning of the round. Join to make a circle for knitting in the round, being careful not to twist the stitches. Knit every round until the hat measures 5½ (6, 6½, 7) inches from the cast-on edge. Next, begin the decrease sequence for the top of the hat.

decrease sequence

Round 1: Knit 6 stitches, knit 2 stitches together. Repeat to the end of the round. 56 (63, 70, 77) stitches remain.

Round 2: Knit 5 stitches, knit 2 stitches together. Repeat to the end of the round. 48 (54, 60, 66) stitches remain.

Round 3: Knit all stitches.

Round 4: Knit onto 3 of the double-pointed needles as follows:

Needle 1: Knit 4 stitches, knit 2 stitches together. Repeat 3 (3, 3, 4) times. 15 (15, 15, 20) stitches are on the first needle.

Needle 2: Knit 4 stitches, knit 2 stitches together. Repeat 3 (3, 3, 4) times. 15 (15, 15, 20) stitches are on the second needle.

Needle 3: Knit 4 stitches, knit 2 stitches together. Repeat 2 (3, 4, 3) times. 10 (15, 20, 15) stitches are on the third needle. 40 (45, 50, 55) total stitches remain.

Use the fourth, or free, double-pointed needle to knit the stitches on each needle for the following rounds.

Round 5: Knit 3 stitches, knit 2 stitches together. Repeat to the end of the round. 32 (36, 40, 44) stitches remain.

The next rounds make the point at the top of the hat.
Rounds 6–10: Knit all stitches.
Round 11: Knit 2 stitches, knit 2 stitches together. Repeat to the end of the round. 24 (27, 30, 33) stitches remain.
Rounds 12–16: Knit all stitches.
Round 17: Knit 1 stitch, knit 2 stitches together. Repeat to the end of the round. 16 (18, 20, 22) stitches remain.
Rounds 18–22: Knit all stitches.
Round 23: Knit 2 stitches together. Repeat to the end of the round. 8 (9, 10, 11) stitches remain.

Change to white and knit as follows:
Rounds 24–28: Knit all stitches.
Round 29: Knit 2 stitches together. Repeat to the end of the round. Knit any remaining stitch. 4 (5, 5, 6) stitches remain.
Round 30: *0–6 month size:* go directly to the knotted I-cord. *6–12 months* and *1–2 years size:* Knit 2 stitches together, knit to the end of the round. 4 stitches remain. *2 years and up size:* Knit 2 stitches together two times, knit to the end of the round. 4 stitches remain.

knotted i-cord
Put the remaining 4 stitches on 1 double-pointed needle. Make a 2-inch I-cord. Bind off.

Cut the yarn, leaving an 8-inch tail, and pull the tail through the remaining stitch. Thread the tail onto a yarn needle, pull it through the middle of the cord to the inside of the hat, and weave in the end. Tie a knot in the I-cord.

sailboat appliqué
For the following appliqué pieces, use 2 of the double-pointed needles as straight needles to knit back and forth.

large sail
With white, use the long-tail method to cast on 9 stitches.
Row 1: Knit all stitches.
Row 2: Knit to the last 2 stitches, knit 2 stitches together. 8 stitches remain.
Row 3: Knit all stitches.
Row 4: Knit to the last 2 stitches, knit 2 stitches together. 7 stitches remain.
Row 5: Knit all stitches.
Row 6: Knit to the last 2 stitches, knit 2 stitches together. 6 stitches remain.
Row 7: Knit all stitches.
Row 8: Knit to the last 2 stitches, knit 2 stitches together. 5 stitches remain.

Row 9: Knit all stitches.
Row 10: Knit to the last 2 stitches, knit 2 stitches together. 4 stitches remain.
Row 11: Knit all stitches.
Row 12: Knit to the last 2 stitches, knit 2 stitches together. 3 stitches remain.
Row 13: Knit 3 stitches together. 1 stitch remains.

Cut the yarn, leaving an 8-inch tail, and pull the tail through the remaining stitch.

small sail

With white, use the long-tail method to cast on 7 stitches.
Row 1: Knit all stitches.
Row 2: Knit to the last 2 stitches, knit 2 stitches together. 6 stitches remain.
Row 3: Knit all stitches.
Row 4: Knit to the last 2 stitches, knit 2 stitches together. 5 stitches remain.
Row 5: Knit all stitches.
Row 6: Knit to the last 2 stitches, knit 2 stitches together. 4 stitches remain.
Row 7: Knit all stitches.
Row 8: Knit to the last 2 stitches, knit 2 stitches together. 3 stitches remain.
Row 9: Knit 3 stitches together.

Cut the yarn, leaving an 8-inch tail, and pull the tail through the remaining stitch.

i-cord

With navy, use the long-tail method to cast on 3 stitches. Make a 2-inch I-cord. Cut the yarn, leaving a 6-inch tail, and pull the tail through the stitches. Weave in the end.

boat

With red, cast on 6 stitches.
Row 1: Knit all stitches.
Row 2: Knit in the front and back of the first stitch, knit 4 stitches, knit in the front and back of the last stitch. 8 stitches.
Row 3: Knit in the front and back of the first stitch, knit 6 stitches, knit in the front and back of the last stitch. 10 stitches.
Row 4: Knit in the front and back of the first stitch, knit 8 stitches, knit in the front and back of the last stitch. 12 stitches.
Row 5: Knit in the front and back of the first stitch, knit 10 stitches, knit in the front and back of the last stitch. 14 stitches.
Row 6: Knit in the front and back of the first stitch, knit 12 stitches, knit in the front and back of the last stitch. 16 stitches.
Row 7: Knit in the front and back of the first stitch, knit 14 stitches, knit in the front and back of the last stitch. 18 stitches.
Row 8: Knit all stitches.
Bind off.

Cut the yarn, leaving an 8-inch tail. Pull the tail through the remaining stitch.

making up

Begin by attaching the boat. Measure up from the bottom of the hat 1½ inches. Pin the boat onto the hat. Thread the boat's tail onto a yarn needle and stitch the boat to the hat. Sew the I-cord above the center of the boat by stitching up and down both sides of the I-cord.
Attach the sails in the same way, pinning them in place before stitching.

Pull all of the ends through to the inside and weave in.

ribbons

There are so many beautiful ribbons available. It would be a crime not to incorporate them with the wonderful yarn we have at our fingertips. You can create a rich variety of colors and textures by adding ribbons to a hat.

When I began making this hat, I pulled the ribbon right through the knitted fabric, which was difficult at times, so I added eyelets to make the weaving of the ribbons easier. If you think four rows of ribbon is too much, put only the first eyelet row in and use a single band of ribbon. This understated version is just as pretty.

HAT

With white and circular needles, use the long-tail method to cast on 64 (72, 80, 88) stitches. Slip a stitch marker onto the right needle to mark the beginning of the round. Join to make a circle for knitting in the round, being careful not to twist the stitches. Knit every round until the hat measures 2 inches from the cast-on edge. Next, begin making the eyelet rounds to thread ribbon through. You will complete four eyelet rounds total.

Knit eyelet rounds as follows:

Round 1: Knit 4 (5, 6, 7) stitches, yarn over, knit 2 stitches together, knit 1 stitch, yarn over, knit 2 stitches together. Repeat to the end of the round.

Rounds 2–4: Knit all stitches.

> **TIP** • When knitting through the yarn over from the previous round, knit through the back of the loop for a more open eyelet.

Round 5: Knit 1 (2, 3, 4) stitch(es), yarn over, knit 2 stitches together, knit 1 stitch, yarn over, knit 2 stitches together, knit 3 stitches. Repeat to the end of the round.

Rounds 6–8: Knit all stitches, following above tip.

Round 9: Repeat round 1.

Rounds 10–12: Knit all stitches, following above tip.

Round 13: Repeat round 5.

Knit every round until the hat measures 5½ (6, 6½, 7) inches from the cast-on edge. Next, begin the decrease sequence for the top of the hat.

decrease sequence

Round 1: Knit 6 stitches, knit 2 stitches together. Repeat to the end of the round. 56 (63, 70, 77) stitches remain.

Round 2: Knit 5 stitches, knit 2 stitches together. Repeat to the end of the round. 48 (54, 60, 66) stitches remain.

Round 3: Knit all stitches.

Round 4: Knit onto 3 of the double-pointed needles as follows:

Needle 1: Knit 4 stitches, knit 2 stitches together. Repeat 3 (3, 3, 4) times. 15 (15, 15, 20) stitches are on the first needle.

Needle 2: Knit 4 stitches, knit 2 stitches together. Repeat 3 (3, 3, 4) times. 15 (15, 15, 20) stitches are on the second needle.

Needle 3: Knit 4 stitches, knit 2 stitches together. Repeat 2 (3, 4, 3) times. 10 (15, 20, 15) stitches are on the third needle. 40 (45, 50, 55) total stitches remain.

Use the fourth, or free, double-pointed needle to knit the stitches on each needle for the following rounds.

Round 5: Knit all stitches.

Round 6: Knit 3 stitches, knit 2 stitches together. Repeat to the end of the round. 32 (36, 40, 44) stitches remain.

Rounds 7 and 8: Knit all stitches.

Round 9: Knit 2 stitches, knit 2 stitches together. Repeat to the end of the round. 24 (27, 30, 33) stitches remain.

Round 10: Knit all stitches.

Round 11: Knit 1 stitch, knit 2 stitches together. Repeat to the end of the round. 16 (18, 20, 22) stitches remain.

Round 12: Knit 2 stitches together. Repeat to the end of the round. 8 (9, 10, 11) stitches remain.

Knit these stitches for 1 inch to make the stem.

Cut the yarn, leaving a 6-inch tail, and thread the tail onto a yarn needle. Pull it through the remaining stitches. Pull tightly to completely close the ring. Weave in the ends on the inside of the hat.

ribbons

Thread ribbon through a yarn needle, if necessary, and pull it through the first row of eyelets on the hat. Leave plenty of excess ribbon between the sets of holes to give stretching room for the hat. If the ribbon is pulled through too tightly, the hat will not fit on the baby's head. Tie the ribbon in a knot when the round is completed. Cut the ends at an angle at the desired length. Repeat weaving the ribbon, row by row, until 4 rows have been completed.

Next, cut four 6-inch strips of ribbon to attach to the stem. Pull the strips through various spots at the base and top of the stem and tie the strips in half-knots.

football

Football is a big deal at my house. My husband played college football and both of my sons, Evan and Ben, play as well. I prefer to knit football hats, like this one. This hat is designed to resemble old-fashioned leather football helmets.

skills needed

- Long-tail cast-on (page 20)
- Knit in the front and back of the same stitch (page 36)
- Knit stitch (page 23)
- Purl stitch (page 25)
- Seed stitch (page 33)
- Backward-loop cast-on (page 22)
- Knitting in the round on circular needles (page 26)
- Knit 2 stitches together (page 36)
- Knitting in the round on double-pointed needles (page 27)
- Single crochet (page 43)
- Slip stitch (page 43)
- Slip knot (page 42)
- Slip stitch, slip stitch, knit 2 stitches together through the back loops (page 35)
- Sewing on an appliqué (page 41)
- Backstitch (page 44)

size

- 0–6 months (6–12 months, 1–2 years, 2 years and up)

yarn

- GGH Samoa (50% cotton/50% microfiber; 104 yards/50 grams), 1(1, 2, 2) skein(s) #91 (light blue)
- Rowan Handknit Cotton (100% cotton; 93 yards/50 grams), 1 skein #253 Tope
- Small amount of white yarn for embroidery

tools

- 16-inch circular needles, U.S. size 7 or size needed to obtain gauge
- Set of 4 double-pointed needles, U.S. size 7 or size needed to obtain gauge
- Stitch marker
- Ruler or tape measure
- Scissors
- Yarn needle
- Crochet hook, U.S. size G
- Pins

gauge

- 4½ stitches per inch

ear flaps (make 2)

With 2 double-pointed needles used as straight needles, knit back and forth. With light blue, use the long-tail method to cast on 8 stitches.

Rows 1–3: Knit in the front and back of the first stitch, work to the last stitch in seed stitch, knit in the front and back of the last stitch. 14 stitches at end of row 3.

Rows 4–6: Work all stitches in seed stitch.

Row 7: Knit in the front and back of the first stitch, work 12 stitches in seed stitch, knit in the front and back of the last stitch. 16 stitches.

Rows 8–16: Work all stitches in seed stitch.

Cut the yarn, leaving a 4-inch tail, and set aside, leaving the stitches on the double-pointed needle. With an empty double-pointed needle, begin second ear flap.

HAT

With circular needles and light blue, use the long-tail method to cast on 7 (9, 11, 13) stitches. Knit across the stitches on the first ear flap, cast on 18 (22, 26, 30) stitches with backward-loop method, knit across the stitches on the second ear flap, cast on 7 (9, 11, 13) stitches with the backward loop method.

64 (72, 80, 88) stitches. Join to make a circle, being careful not to twist the stitches. Place a stitch marker on the right needle to show the beginning of the round. Work in seed stitch for 4 rounds. Then knit every round until the hat measures 4 (4½, 5, 6) inches from the cast-on edge. Next, begin the decrease sequence for the top of the hat.

decrease sequence

Round 1: Knit 6 stitches, knit 2 stitches together. Repeat to the end of the round. 56 (63, 70, 77) stitches remain.

Round 2: Knit 5 stitches, knit 2 stitches together. Repeat to the end of the round. 48 (54, 60, 66) stitches remain.

Round 3: Knit all stitches.

Round 4: Knit onto 3 of the double-pointed needles as follows:

Needle 1: Knit 4 stitches, knit 2 stitches together. Repeat 3 (3, 3, 4) times. 15 (15, 15, 20) stitches are on the first needle.

Needle 2: Knit 4 stitches, knit 2 stitches together. Repeat 3 (3, 3, 4) times. 15 (15, 15, 20) stitches are on the second needle.

Needle 3: Knit 4 stitches, knit 2 stitches together. Repeat 2 (3, 4, 3) times. 10 (15, 20, 15) stitches are on the third needle. 40 (45, 50, 55) total stitches remain.

Use the fourth, or free, double-pointed needle to knit the stitches on each needle for the following rounds.

Round 5: Knit all stitches.

Round 6: Knit 3 stitches, knit 2 stitches together. Repeat to the end of the round. 32 (36, 40, 44) stitches remain.

Rounds 7 and 8: Knit all stitches.

Round 9: Knit 2 stitches, knit 2 stitches together. Repeat to the end of the round. 24 (27, 30, 33) stitches remain.

Round 10: Knit all stitches.

Round 11: Knit 1 stitch, knit 2 stitches together. Repeat to the end of the round. 16 (18, 20, 22) stitches remain.

Round 12: Knit 2 stitches together. Repeat to the end of the round. 8 (9, 10, 11) stitches remain.

edging

Starting at the back of the hat with the crochet hook and Tope, single crochet around the edge of the hat. Join the round with a slip stitch. Cut the yarn and weave in the end.

football

Use 2 of the double-pointed needles as straight needles to knit back and forth. With Tope, make a slip knot on the needle.

Row 1: Knit in the front and back of the slip knot. 2 stitches.

Row 2 and all even rows: Purl.

Row 3: Knit in the front and back of each of the two stitches. 4 stitches.

Row 5: Knit in the front and back of the first stitch, knit 2 stitches, knit in the front and back of the remaining stitch. 6 stitches.

Row 7: Knit in the front and back of the first stitch, knit 4 stitches, knit in the front and back of the remaining stitch. 8 stitches.

Row 9: Knit all stitches.

Row 11: Slip 1 stitch, slip 1 stitch, knit the slipped stitches together through the back loops, knit 4 stitches, knit 2 stitches together. 6 stitches remain.

Row 13: Slip 1 stitch, slip 1 stitch, knit the slipped stitches together through the back loops, knit 2 stitches, knit 2 stitches together. 4 stitches remain.

Row 15: Slip 1 stitch, slip 1 stitch, knit the slipped stitches together through the back of the loops, knit 2 stitches together. 2 stitches remain. Do not turn.

Pass the 2nd stitch over the 1st stitch. Cut the yarn, leaving an 8-inch tail. Pull the tail through the remaining stitch.

making up

Pin the football in place on the center front of the hat. Thread the tail onto a yarn needle and sew the football onto the hat. With the yarn needle and white, embroider football markings on the football using backstitch.

sprout

Cut an 18-inch strand of white and thread it onto a yarn needle. At the top point of the hat, make ten 1½ inch loops using your pointer finger as a loop holder and going through the same spot onto hat. Cut a 12-inch strand of Tope and thread it onto the yarn needle. Wrap the yarn tightly around the base of the loops, leaving ½ inch of white sticking out at the top. Pull all the ends through to the inside of the hat and weave in. Cut the loops at the top of the sprout and trim.

inca snowflake

Kureyon is a beautiful yarn with a rich color palette in many different colorways. The only problem with it is that, for many children, it is just too scratchy to wear. I still cannot resist knitting with this yarn for children because of the color selection. The simple solution to scratchy wool is to add a fleece lining to the hat. Fleece is easy to cut and sew, and it comes in lots of colors. It also adds great warmth to any hat. If you are lucky enough to have a child whom wool doesn't scratch, feel free to make this hat without the lining.

I have always loved the Inca-style hat, especially the way the flaps keep little ears warm. The tassels on the flaps are made to be decorative, but if you make the braids longer, they can be used for ties as well.

skills needed

- Long-tail cast-on (page 20)
- Knit in the front and back of the same stitch (page 36)
- Knit stitch (page 23)
- Purl stitch (page 25)
- Purl in the front and back of the same stitch (page 36)
- Stockinette stitch (page 32)
- Backward-loop cast-on (page 22)
- Knitting in the round on circular needles (page 26)
- Knit 2 stitches together (page 35)
- Single crochet (page 43)
- Slip stitch (page 43)
- Backstitch (page 44)
- Tassels (page 48)
- Whipstitch (page 41)

size

- 3–18 months (18–24 months, 2 years and up)

yarn

- Noro Kureyon (100% wool; 110 yards/ 50 grams), 1 (2, 2) skeins of variegated #95
- Classic Elite Montera (50% llama/50% wool; 127 yards/100 grams), 1 skein #3816 Lapaz Natural

tools

- 16-inch circular needles, U.S. size 7 or size needed to obtain gauge
- Set of 4 double-pointed needles, U.S. size 7 or size needed to obtain gauge
- Stitch marker
- Ruler or tape measure
- Scissosrs
- Yarn needle
- Crochet hook, U.S. size G

optional

- ¼ yard of fleece for lining
- Sewing needle and thread
- Pins

gauge

- 5 stitches per inch

ear flaps (make 2)

Use 2 of the double-pointed needles as straight needles to knit back and forth. With Kureyon, use the long-tail method to cast on 8 stitches.

Row 1: Knit in the front and back of the first stitch, knit 6 stitches, knit in the front and back of the remaining stitch. 10 stitches.

Row 2: Purl in the front and back of the first stitch, purl 8 stitches, purl in the front and back of the remaining stitch. 12 stitches.

Row 3: Knit in the front and back of the first stitch, knit 10 stitches, knit in the front and back of the remaining stitch. 14 stitches.

Row 4: Purl all stitches.

Row 5: Knit all stitches.

Row 6: Purl all stitches.

Row 7: Knit in the front and back of the first stitch, knit 12 stitches, knit in the front and back of the remaining stitch. 16 stitches.

Rows 8–16: Work in stockinette stitch starting with a purl row.

Cut the yarn, leaving a 4-inch tail, and set aside, leaving the stitches on a double-pointed needle.

HAT

With circular needles and Kureyon, use the long-tail method to cast on 9 (11, 13) stitches. Knit across the stitches on the first ear flap, cast on 22 (26, 30) stitches using the backward-loop method, knit across the second ear flap, cast on 9 (11, 13) stitches using the backward-loop method. 72 (80, 88) stitches. Slip a stitch marker onto the right needle to show the beginning of the round. Join to make a circle for knitting in the round, being careful not to twist the stitches.

Knit every round until the hat measures 4½ (5, 6) inches from the cast-on edge. Next, begin the decrease sequence for the top of the hat.

decrease sequence

Round 1: Knit 6 stitches, knit 2 stitches together. Repeat to the end of the round. 63 (70, 77) stitches remain.

Round 2: Knit 5 stitches, knit 2 stitches together. Repeat to the end of the round. 54 (60, 66) stitches remain.

Rounds 3–9: Knit all stitches.

Round 10: Knit onto 3 of the double-pointed needles as follows:

Needle 1: Knit 4 stitches, knit 2 stitches together. Repeat 3 (3, 4) times. 15 (15, 20) stitches are on the first needle.

Needle 2: Knit 4 stitches, knit 2 stitches together. Repeat 3 (3, 4) times. 15 (15, 20) stitches are on the second needle.

Needle 3: Knit 4 stitches, knit 2 stitches together. Repeat 3 (4, 3) times. 15 (20, 15) stitches are on the third needle. 45 (50, 55) total stitches remain.

Use the fourth, or free, double-pointed needle to knit the stitches on each needle for the following rounds.

Rounds 11–24: Knit all stitches.

Round 25: Knit 3 stitches, knit 2 stitches together. Repeat to the end of the round. 36 (40, 44) stitches remain.

Round 26: Knit all stitches.

Round 27: Knit 2 stitches, knit 2 stitches together. Repeat to the end of the round. 27 (30, 33) stitches remain.

Round 28: Knit all stitches.

Round 29: Knit 1 stitch, knit 2 stitches together. Repeat to the end of the round. 18 (20, 22) stitches remain.

Round 30: Knit 2 stitches together. Repeat to the end of the round. 9 (10, 11) stitches remain.

Cut the yarn, leaving a 6-inch tail, and thread the tail onto a yarn needle. Pull it through the remaining stitches. Pull tightly to completely close the ring. Weave in the tail on the inside of the hat.

edging
With Montera and the crochet hook, single crochet around the bottom edge, joining the round with a slip stitch. Cut the yarn and pull it through the remaining stitch. Weave in the end.

snowflake embroidery
With Montera and the yarn needle, embroider snowflakes in backstitch. Use the photograph as a guide, but make up your own original snowflakes, too.

tassels
Cut six 24-inch strands of Kureyon and set aside. Cut three 12-inch strands of Kureyon and set aside.

With Montera, make three 2-inch tassels with 20 wraps each. Cut the loops and trim the ends.

Take three of the 24-inch strands of Kureyon and pull them through the uncut end of a tassel until the ends are even. Tie a half-knot to secure. Divide the strands into three groups of two strands each and braid for 4 inches. Tie a knot to secure. Using one tail and the yarn needle, sew the braided end to the inside of one ear flap. Trim the ends.

Repeat for the other ear flap.

Repeat for the third tassel, using the 12-inch strands and braiding for 1½ inches. Pull the ends of the strands through the top center and secure on the inside of the hat. Cut the ends and weave them in.

optional fleece lining
Fold the ¼-yard piece of fleece in half. Using the knitted hat as a pattern, place the hat (laid flat so the ear flaps line up one on top of the other) on the fleece with the front of the hat lining up with the fold line of the fleece. Pin the hat in place on the fleece. Cut the fleece around the hat, cutting just slightly inside the outer edge of the hat. One inch down from the top of the hat, cut the fleece straight across.

With a sewing needle and thread, use whipstitch to sew the back seam of the lining. Slide the lining into the hat and sew the bottom edge of the fleece to the hat just inside the crocheted edging. Now the hat is attached around the bottom edge of the hat and the ear flaps. Turn the hat inside out and smooth the lining. Sew the top of the fleece lining to the hat about 1 inch from the top. Turn the hat right side out.

snowman

Snowmen have been a longtime love of mine. We have many heavy snowfalls in Wisconsin, and almost every front yard has a snowman. Of all my snowman designs, this version is my favorite.

skills needed

- Long-tail cast-on (page 20)
- Knit stitch (page 23)
- Knitting in the round on circular needles (page 26)
- Purl stitch (page 25)
- Knit 2 stitches together (page 35)
- Knitting in the round on double-pointed needles (page 27)
- Garter stitch (page 32)
- Bind off (page 30)
- Whipstitch (page 41)
- Slip knot (page 42)
- Knit in the front and back of the same stitch (page 36)
- Slip stitch, slip stitch, knit 2 stitches together through the back loops (page 35)
- Fringe (page 49)
- Running stitch (page 45)

size

- Newborn (0–6 months, 6–18 months, 1–2 years, 2 years and up)

yarn

- GGH Samoa (50% cotton/50% microfiber; 104 yards/50 grams), 1 skein #18 (white)
- Rowan Handknit Cotton (100% cotton; 93 yards/ 50 grams), 1 skein #252 Black, small amounts of #215 Rosso and #254 Flame

tools

- 16-inch circular needles, U.S. size 7 or size needed to obtain gauge
- Set of 4 double-pointed needles, U.S. size 7 or size needed to obtain gauge
- Stitch marker
- Ruler or tape measure
- Scissors
- Yarn needle

gauge

- 4½ stitches per inch

HAT

With circular needles and white, use the long-tail method to cast on 56 (64, 72, 80, 88) stitches, leaving a 10-inch tail. Slip a stitch marker onto the right needle to show the beginning of the round. Join to make a circle for knitting in the round, being careful not to twist the stitches. Knit until the hat measures 1 inch from the cast-on edge. Purl 1 round for the turning row. Knit until the hat measures 3½ (3¾, 4, 4½, 4¾) inches from the turning row. Change to black. Knit 1 round. Purl 1 round. Knit all rounds for 2 inches. Purl 1 round. Next, begin the decrease sequence for the top of the hat.

decrease sequence

Round 1: Knit 6 stitches, knit 2 stitches together. Repeat to the end of the round. 49 (56, 63, 70, 77) stitches remain.

Rounds 2 and 3: Knit all stitches.

Round 4: Knit 5 stitches, knit 2 stitches together. Repeat to the end of the round. 42 (48, 54, 60, 66) stitches remain.

Rounds 5 and 6: Knit all stitches.

Round 7: Knit onto 3 of the double-pointed needles as follows:

Needle 1: Knit 4 stitches, knit 2 stitches together. Repeat 2 (3, 3, 3, 4) times. 10 (15, 15, 15, 20) stitches are on the first needle.

Needle 2: Knit 4 stitches, knit 2 stitches together. Repeat 2 (3, 3, 3, 4) times. 10 (15, 15, 15, 20) stitches are on the second needle.
Needle 3: Knit 4 stitches, knit 2 stitches together. Repeat 3 (2, 3, 4, 3) times. 15 (10, 15, 20, 15) stitches are on the third needle. 35 (40, 45, 50, 55) total stitches remain.

Use the fourth, or free, double-pointed needle to knit the stitches on each needle for the following rounds.
Rounds 8 and 9: Knit all stitches.
Round 10: Knit 3 stitches, knit 2 stitches together. Repeat to the end of the round. 28 (32, 36, 40, 44) stitches remain.
Round 11: Knit 2 stitches, knit 2 stitches together. Repeat to the end of the round. 21 (24, 27, 30, 33) stitches remain.
Round 12: Knit 1 stitch, knit 2 stitches together. Repeat to the end of the round. 14 (16, 18, 20, 22) stitches remain.
Round 13: Knit 2 stitches together. Repeat to the end of the round. 7 (8, 9, 10, 11) stitches remain.

Cut the yarn, leaving a 6-inch length tail, and thread the tail onto a yarn needle. Pull it through the remaining stitches. Pull tightly to completely close the ring. Weave in the ends on the inside of the hat.

brim

Use 2 of the double-pointed needles as straight needles to knit back and forth. With black, use the long-tail method to cast on 5 stitches. Knit in garter stitch until the brim fits around the hat, measuring as you knit. Bind off, leaving a 12-inch tail. Sew the brim to the hat at the first black purl row with whipstitch, yarn needle, and tail.

eyes (make 2)

Use 2 of the double-pointed needles as straight needles to knit back and forth. With black, make a slip knot, leaving a 4-inch tail.

Row 1: Knit in the front and back of the slip knot until 5 stitches are on the right needle.
Row 2: Knit all stitches.
Row 3: Purl all stitches.
Row 4: Knit all stitches. Do not turn.
Pass the 2nd, 3rd, 4th, 5th stitches over the 1st stitch. Cut the yarn, leaving a 6-inch tail, and pull the tail through the remaining stitch. Thread the 6-inch tail onto a yarn needle, stuff the bobble with the 4-inch tail from the slip knot, gather up, and secure with the remaining tail.

carrot nose

Use 2 of the double-pointed needles as straight needles to knit back and forth. With Flame, use the long-tail method to cast on 9 stitches.
Row 1 and all odd rows: Knit all stitches.
Row 2: Slip 1 stitch, slip 1 stitch, knit 2 stitches together through the back loops, knit 7 stitches, knit 2 stitches together. 7 stitches remain.
Row 4: Slip 1 stitch, slip 1 stitch, knit 2 stitches together through the back loops, knit 5 stitches, knit 2 stitches together. 5 stitches remain.
Row 6: Slip 1 stitch, slip 1 stitch, knit 2 stitches together through the back loops, knit 3 stitches, knit 2 stitches together. 3 stitches remain.
Row 8: Knit 3 stitches, pass the 2nd and 3rd stitches over the 1st stitch.
Cut the yarn, leaving a 6-inch tail, and pull the tail through last the stitch.
Sew the seam and leave a tail for sewing onto the hat.

scarf

Use 2 of the double-pointed needles as straight needles to knit back and forth. With Rosso, use the long-tail method to, cast on 5 stitches. Work in garter stitch until the scarf measures 20 (21, 22, 23, 24) inches from the cast-on edge. Bind off, leaving a 12-inch tail.

fringe

Cut twelve 3-inch pieces of red. Put 6 pieces of fringe on each end of the scarf, holding 2 pieces of yarn together for each fringe. Trim to make ends even.

making up

Fold the bottom of the hat under at the turning row. Thread the tail onto a yarn needle. Sew it to the inside of the hat using whipstitch.

Attach the scarf to the hat using the hem seam as a guide. Place the center of the scarf at the seam on the right side of the hat. Thread the scarf tail onto a yarn needle. Attach the scarf with running stitch. Leave the ends loose and tie in a half-knot to the side of where the face will be.

In the space between the scarf and the brim, attach the eyes and carrot nose using the yarn needle and the remaining tails.

jumping child

When I was working for a manufacturing company, one of my first assignments was to make a hat with children as the motif. I made a hat using different colors and children knitted into the fabric using intarsia. When I presented the design to the company, they sent me back to the drawing board. Then I came up with the appliqué version of the child. The design came to life and had much more energy and interest. The company loved it.

Part of the fun of making knitted appliqués is that the fabric is so flexible, you can stretch your appliqué into many different shapes as you sew it on. The pattern is written using the blue hat coloring, but the red hat yarn information is provided.

skills needed

- Long-tail cast-on (page 20)
- Knit stitch (page 23)
- Knitting in the round on circular needles (page 26)
- Knit 2 stitches together (page 35)
- Knitting in the round on double-pointed needles (page 27)
- Backward-loop cast-on (page 22)
- Bind off (page 30)
- Joining yarn (page 38)
- Knit in the front and back of the same stitch (page 36)
- Slip stitch, slip stitch, knit 2 stitches together through the back loops (page 35)
- Sewing on an appliqué (page 41)
- Satin stitch (page 44)

size

- 0–6 months (6–12 months, 1–2 years, 2 years and up)

yarn

- RYC Cashcotton DK (35% cotton/25% polyamide/18% angora/13% viscose/9% cashmere; 142 yards/50 grams), 1 skein #601 Cool, small amounts of #605 Magenta and #603 Apple
- Rowan Handknit Cotton (100% cotton; 93 yards/50 grams), small amounts of #205 Linen and #252 Black
- Tahki Cotton Classic (100% cotton; 108 yards/50 grams), small amount of #3525 (yellow)

red hat colorway

- Provence (100% mercerized Egyptian cotton; 100 yards/100 grams) 1 skein #2627 French Red, small amounts of #2678 Portabello, #2673 Maize, #2657 Denimes Blue, and #2613 Black

tools

- 16-inch circular needles, U.S. size 7 or size needed to obtain gauge
- Set of 4 double-pointed needles, U.S. size 7 or size needed to obtain gauge
- 2 double-pointed needles, U.S. size 5 (for appliqué)
- Pins
- Stitch marker
- Ruler or tape measure
- Scissors
- Yarn needle

gauge

- 5 stitches per inch

HAT

With circular needles and Cool, use the long-tail method to cast on 64 (72, 80, 88) stitches. Slip a stitch marker onto the right needle to mark the beginning of the round. Join to make a circle for knitting in the round, being careful not to twist the stitches. Knit until the hat measures 5½ (6, 6½, 7) inches from the cast-on edge. Next, begin the decrease sequence for the top of the hat.

decrease sequence

Round 1: Knit 6 stitches, knit 2 stitches together. Repeat to the end of the round. 56 (63, 70, 77) stitches remain.

Round 2: Knit 5 stitches, knit 2 stitches together. Repeat to the end of the round. 48 (54, 60, 66) stitches remain.

Round 3: Knit directly onto 3 of the double-pointed needles as follows:

Needle 1: Knit 4 stitches, knit 2 stitches together. Repeat 3 (3, 3, 4) times. 15 (15, 15, 20) stitches are on the first needle.

Needle 2: Knit 4 stitches, knit 2 stitches together. Repeat 3 (3, 3, 4) times. 15 (15, 15, 20) stitches ar on the second needle.

Needle 3: Knit 4 stitches, knit 2 stitches together. Repeat 2 (3, 4 3) times. 10 (15, 20, 15) stitches are on the third needle. 40 (45, 50, 55) total stitches remain.

Use the fourth, or free, double-pointed needle to knit the stitches on each needle for the following rounds.

Round 4: Knit 3 stitches, knit 2 stitches together. Repeat to the end of the round. 32 (36, 40, 44) stitches remain.

Rounds 5–9: Knit all stitches.

Round 10: Knit 2 stitches, knit 2 stitches together. Repeat to the end of the round. 24 (27, 30, 32) stitches remain.

Rounds 11–15: Knit all stitches.

Round 16: Knit 1 stitch, knit 2 stitches together. Repeat to the end of the round. 16 (18, 20, 22) stitches remain.

Rounds 17–21: Knit all stitches.

Round 22: Knit 2 stitches together. Repeat to the end of the round. 9 (10, 11, 12) stitches remain.

Rounds 23–27: Knit all stitches.

Cut the yarn, leaving a 6-inch tail, and thread the tail onto a yarn needle. Pull it through the remaining stitches. Pull tightly to completely close the ring. Weave in the ends on the inside of the hat.

sprout

Cut an 18-inch strand of Magenta and thread it onto a yarn needle. At the top point of the hat, make ten 1½ inch loops, using your pointer finger as the loop holder and going through the same spot on the hat. Cut a 12-inch strand of Apple and thread it onto a yarn needle. Wrap the strand tightly around the base of the loops, leaving ½ inch of Magenta poking out at the top.

Cut the loops at the top of the sprout and trim.

child appliqué

The child is made in 3 pieces: shirt, pants, and head. After sewing the appliqué in place, add the hair, hands, and shoes.

shirt • With Magenta and using the 2 size 5 double-pointed needles as straight needles, use the long-tail method to cast on 8 stitches.

Row 7: Knit every row for 6 rows. Knit to the end and use the backward-loop method to cast on 6 stitches.

Row 8: Knit to the end and use the backward-loop method to cast on 6 stitches. 20 total stitches.

Rows 9–12: Knit all stitches.

Bind off, leaving an 8-inch tail for attaching the shirt to the hat.

pants • With Apple and using the 2 size 5 double-pointed needles as straight needles, cast on 8 stitches.

Rows 1–4: Knit every stitch.

Row 5: Knit 4 stitches and turn, leaving the remaining stitches on the needle. Working on the first 4 stitches only, knit 20 rows. Bind off.

Rejoin the yarn at the inner edge and knit the remaining 4 stitches. Knit 20 rows and bind off, leaving an 8-inch tail for attaching the pants to the hat.

head • With Linen and using the size 5 2 double-pointed needles as straight needles, cast on 3 stitches.

Rows 1 and 2: Knit every stitch.

Row 3: Knit in the front and the back of the same stitch, knit 1 stitch, knit in the front and the back of the remaining stitch. 5 stitches.

Row 4: Knit in the front and the back of the same stitch, knit 3 stitches, knit in the front and the back of the remaining stitch. 7 stitches.

Rows 5 and 6: Knit every stitch.

Row 7: Slip 1 stitch, slip 1 stitch, knit the slipped stitches together through the back loops, knit 3 stitches, knit 2 stitches together. 5 stitches remain.

Row 8: Slip 1 stitch, slip 1 stitch, knit the slipped stitches together through the back loops, knit 1 stitch, knit 2 stitches together. 3 stitches remain.

Bind off, leaving a 6-inch tail to attach the head to the hat.

making up

Pin the head, shirt, and pants to the front of the hat. Using a yarn needle and the tail of each piece, sew the head, shirt, and pants to the hat.

hair

Cut twenty 2-inch strands of yellow. Hold 2 strands together and thread them onto a yarn needle. Pull the strands through around the hairline of the head and tie them in a half-knot to secure. When all of the strands are in place, separate them into pony tails and tie each one with small piece of Magenta.

To create a different version of the child, cut the hair short.

hands and shoes

Cut an 8-inch strand of Linen for the hands and thread it onto a needle. Create the hands by making 6 small satin stitches at the ends of the arms.

Using black, do the same for shoes.

Pull all ends through to the inside and weave in.

loopy

Texture created with yarn is beautiful and interesting. You can create an incredible variety of looks just by changing the yarn. I created two different versions of Loopy, one using RYC Cashcotton DK (as in this pattern) and the other using Rowan Handknit Cotton in black (#252) for the hat and leftover Colinette Giotto ribbon for the loop rounds. Many of us have leftover yarn from the scarf knitting trend of the last couple of years, and this is the perfect way to use up that fantastic yarn. This hat is fun to make and, once again, is easier than it looks.

skills needed

- Long-tail cast-on (page 20)
- Knit stitch (page 23)
- Knitting in the round on circular needles (page 26)
- Purl stitch (page 25)
- Knit 2 stitches together (page 25)
- Knitting in the round on double-pointed needles (page 27)
- Single crochet (page 43)

size

- Newborn (0–6 months, 6–12 months, 1–2 years)

yarn

- RYC Cashcotton DK (35% cotton/25% polyamide/18% angora/13% viscose/9% cashmere; 142 yards/50 grams), 1 skein each of #606 Quartz, #605 Magenta, #603 Apple, and #601 Cool

tools

- 16-inch circular needle, U.S. size 7 or size needed to obtain gauge
- Set of 4 double-pointed needles, U.S. size 7 or size needed to obtain gauge
- Stitch marker
- Ruler or tape measure
- Scissors
- Yarn needle
- Crochet hook, U.S. size G

gauge

- 5 stitches per inch

HAT

With circular needles and Quartz, use the long-tail method to cast on 64 (72, 80, 88) stitches. Slip a stitch marker onto the right needle to mark the beginning of the round. Join to make a circle for knitting in the round, being careful not to twist the stitches. Knit until the hat measures 1½ inches from the cast-on edge. Next, begin the stitch pattern.

stitch pattern

Round 1: Purl all stitches.
Rounds 2–7: Knit all stitches.
Repeat rounds 1–7 until the hat measures 5½ (6, 6½, 7) inches from the cast-on edge. Next, begin the decrease sequence for the top of the hat.

decrease sequence

Round 1: Knit 6 stitches, knit 2 stitches together. Repeat to the end of the round. 56 (63, 70, 77) stitches remain.
Round 2: Knit 5 stitches, knit 2 stitches together. Repeat to the end of the round. 48 (54, 60, 66) stitches remain.
Round 3: Knit all stitches.
Round 4: Knit onto 3 of the double-pointed needles as follows:
Needle 1: Knit 4 stitches, knit 2 stitches together. Repeat 3 (3, 3, 4) times. 15 (15, 15, 20) stitches are on the first needle.
Needle 2: Knit 4 stitches, knit 2 stitches together. Repeat 3 (3, 3, 4) times. 15 (15, 15, 20) stitches are on the second needle.

Needle 3: Knit 4 stitches, knit 2 stitches together. Repeat 2 (3, 4, 3) times. 10 (15, 20 15) stitches are on the third needle. 40 (45, 40, 55) total stitches remain.

Use the fourth, or free, double-pointed needle to knit the stitches on each needle for the following rounds.

Round 5: Knit all stitches.

Round 6: Knit 3 stitches, knit 2 stitches together. Repeat to the end of the round. 32 (36, 40, 44) stitches remain.

Rounds 7 and 8: Knit all stitches.

Round 9: Knit 2 stitches, knit 2 stitches together. Repeat to the end of the round. 24 (27, 30, 33) stitches remain.

Round 10: Knit all stitches.

Round 11: Knit 1 stitch, knit 2 stitches together. Repeat to the end of the round. 16 (18, 20, 22) stitches remain.

Round 12: Knit 2 stitches together. Repeat to the end of the round. 8 (9, 10, 11) stitches remain.

Cut the yarn, leaving a 6-inch tail, and thread the tail onto a yarn needle. Pull it through the remaining stitches. Pull tightly to competely close the ring. Weave in the ends on the inside of the hat.

sprout

Cut an 18-inch strand of Apple and thread it onto a yarn needle. At the top point of the hat, make ten 1½-inch loops, using your pointer finger as the loop holder and going through the same spot on the hat. Cut a 12-inch strand of Cool and thread it onto the yarn needle. Wrap the yarn tightly around the base of the loops, leaving ½ inch of the Apple loops sticking out at the top.

loops

Foundation round: With the crochet hook and Cool, single crochet through each stitch on the purl round. Next, make the loops on the single crochet round just completed.

Loops: Put the crochet hook through the next single crochet. Wrap the yarn from front to back over your left index finger, making a 1-inch loop. With both strands at the bottom of the hook, pull both through the stitch. With three stitches on the hook, yarn over and draw through all of the stitches. Repeat in each single crochet for the entire round. Don't worry if the loops aren't exactly the same length; it will make the hat look even better.

Switch colors for each purl round and repeat colors as needed.

stars

This style of hat is easy to knit because there is no shaping and the 3-needle bind-off is so slick. This bind-off creates the seam at the top of the hat. Make sure you remember to turn the hat inside out before starting the bind-off. The stars are texturally interesting and not as difficult as they appear. They do require weaving in ends, but the result is well worth it.

skills needed

- Long-tail cast-on (page 20)
- Knit stitch (page 23)
- Knitting in the round on circular needles (page 26)
- Purl stitch (page 25)
- Seed stitch (page 33)
- 3-needle bind-off (page 31)
- Slip knot (page 42)
- Knit in the front and back of the same stitch (page 36)
- Knit 2 stitches together (page 35)
- Knitting in the round on double-pointed needles (page 27)
- French knots (page 46)
- Sewing on an appliqué (page 41)
- Tassels (page 48)

size

- Newborn (0–6 months, 6–12 months, 1–2 years, 2 years and up)

yarn

- GGH Samoa (50% cotton/50% microfiber; 104 yards/50 grams), 1 skein each of #18 (white), #5 (yellow), #85 (light blue), and #56 (dark blue)

tools

- 16-inch circular needles, U.S. size 7 or size needed to obtain gauge
- Set of 4 double-pointed needles, U.S. size 7 or size needed to obtain gauge
- Stitch marker
- Ruler or tape measure
- Scissors
- Yarn needle

gauge

- 5 stitches per inch

HAT

With circular needles and yellow, use the long-tail method to cast on 56 (64, 72, 80, 88) stitches. Slips a stitch marker onto the right needle to mark the beginning of the round. Join to make a circle for knitting in the round, being careful not to twist the stitches. Work seed stitch for 4 rounds. Then knit until the hat measures 4½ (5, 5½, 6, 6½) inches from the cast-on edge. **Turn the hat inside out.** Divide the stitches in half, placing one half on a separate needle. Use the 3-needle bind-off to finish. Turn the hat right-side out.

large star

points (make 5) • With light blue and 2 double-pointed needles used as straight needles to knit back and forth, make a slip knot.
Row 1: Knit in the front and back of the slip knot. 2 stitches.
Row 2 (and all even rows): Knit all stitches.
Row 3: Knit in the front and back of the same stitch in each of the two stitches. 4 stitches.
Row 5: Knit in the front and back of the first stitch, knit 2 stitches, knit in the front and back of the last stitch. 6 stitches.
Row 7: Knit in the front and back of the first stitch, knit 4 stitches, knit in the front and back of the last stitch. 8 stitches.
Row 9: Knit in the front and back of the first stitch, knit 6 stitches, knit in the front and back of the last stitch. 10 stitches.
Row 10: Knit all stitches.

Cut the yarn, leaving a 6-inch tail. Leave the stitches on the double-pointed needle and set aside. Slip the 4 subsequent points onto the set-aside double-pointed needle. 5 points (50 stitches total) on the needle.

center • Pick up the double-pointed needle holding the 5 points and 50 stitches and, knitting onto 3 of the double-pointed needles, knit 1 row, dividing the stitches as follows:
Needle 1: 16 stitches.
Needle 2: 16 stitches.
Needle 3: 18 stitches.
Join the round, being careful not to twist the stitches.
Use the fourth, or free, double-pointed needle to knit the stitches on each needle for the following rounds.
Round 1: Knit 2 stitches together. Repeat to the end of the round. 25 stitches remain.
Rounds 2 and 3: Knit all stitches.
Round 4: Knit 2 stitches together. Repeat to last the last 3 stitches. Knit 3 stitches together. 12 stitches remain.
Round 5: Knit all stitches.
Round 6: Knit 2 stitches together. Repeat to the end of the round. 6 stitches remain.

Cut the yarn, leaving a 6-inch tail, and thread the tail onto a yarn needle. Pull it through the remaining stitches. Pull tightly to completely close the ring. Weave in the end on the knit side. (Purl side is the right side.)

medium star
points (make 5) • With white and 2 double-pointed needles used as straight needles to knit back and forth, make a slip knot.
Row 1: Knit in the front and back of the slip knot. 2 stitches.
Row 2 (and all even rows): Knit all stitches.
Row 3: Knit in the front and back of the same stitch in each of the two stitches. 4 stitches.

Row 5: Knit in the front and back of the first stitch, knit 2 stitches, knit in the front and back of the last stitch. 6 stitches.
Row 7: Knit in the front and back of the first stitch, knit 4 stitches, knit in the front and back of the last stitch. 8 stitches.
Row 8: Knit all stitches.

Cut the yarn, leaving a 6-inch tail. Leave the stitches on the double-pointed needle and set aside. Slip the 4 subsequent points onto the set-aside double-pointed needle. 5 points (40 stitches total) on the needle.

center • Pick up the double-pointed needle holding the 5 points and 40 stitches and, knitting onto 3 double-pointed needles, knit 1 row, dividing the stitches as follows:
Needle 1: 14 stitches.
Needle 2: 14 stitches.
Needle 3: 12 stitches.
Join the round, being careful not to twist the stitches.
Use the fourth, or free, double-pointed needle to knit the stitches on each needle for the following rounds.
Round 1: Knit 2 stitches together. Repeat to the end of the round. 20 stitches remain.
Rounds 2 and 3: Knit all stitches.
Round 4: Knit 2 stitches together. Repeat to the end of the round. 10 stitches remain.
Round 5: Knit all stitches.
Round 6: Knit 2 stitches together to the last stitch. Repeat to the end of the round. 5 stitches remain.

Cut the yarn, leaving a 6-inch tail, and thread the tail onto a yarn needle. Pull it through the remaining stitches. Pull tightly to completely close the ring. Weave in the end on the knit side. (Purl side is the right side.)

little star
points (make 5) • With light blue and 2 double-pointed needles used as straight needles to knit back and forth, make a slip knot.

Row 1: Knit in the front and back of the slip knot. 2 stitches.

Rows 2 and 4: Knit all stitches.

Row 3: Knit in the front and back of the same stitch in each of the 2 stitches. 4 stitches.

Row 5: Knit in the front and back of the first stitch, knit 2 stitches, knit in the front and back of the last stitch. 6 stitches.

Row 6: Knit all stitches.

Cut the yarn, leaving a 6-inch tail. Leave the stitches on the double-pointed needle and set aside. Slip the 4 subsequent points onto the set-aside double-pointed needle. 5 points (30 stitches total) on the needle.

center • Pick up the double-pointed needle holding the 5 points and 30 stitches and, knitting onto 3 of the double-pointed needles, knit 1 row, dividing the stitches evenly with 10 stitches on each needle.

Join the round, being careful not to twist the stitches.

Use the fourth, or free, double-pointed needle to knit the stitches on each needle for the following rounds.

Round 1: Knit 2 stitches together. Repeat to the end of the round. 15 stitches remain.

Round 2: Knit all stitches.

Round 3: Knit 2 stitches together, knit 1 stitch, knit 2 stitches together. 9 stitches remain.

Cut the yarn, leaving a 6-inch tail, and thread the tail onto a yarn needle. Pull it through the remaining stitches. Pull tightly to completely close the ring. Weave in the end on the knit side. (Purl side is the right side.)

tiny star

points (make 5) • With dark blue and 2 double-pointed needles used as straight needles to knit back and forth, make a slip knot.

Row 1: Knit in the front and back of the slip knot. 2 stitches.

Row 2: Knit all stitches.

Row 3: Knit in the front and back of the same stitch in each of the 2 stitches. 4 stitches.

Row 4: Knit all stitches.

Cut the yarn, leaving a 6-inch tail. Leave the stitches on the double-pointed needle and set aside. Slip the 4 subsequent points onto the set-aside double-pointed needle. 5 points (20 stitches total) on the needle.

center • Pick up the double-pointed needle holding the 5 points and 20 stitches and, knitting onto 3 double-pointed needles, knit 1 row, dividing the stitches as follows:

Needle 1: 6 stitches.

Needle 2: 7 stitches.

Needle 3: 7 stitches.

Join the round, being careful not to twist the stitches.

Use the fourth, or free, double-pointed needle to knit the stitches on each needle for the following round.

Round 1: Knit 2 stitches together. Repeat to the end of the round. 10 stitches remain.

Cut the yarn, leaving a 6-inch tail, and thread the tail onto a yarn needle. Pull it through the remaining stitches. Pull tightly to completely close the ring. Weave in the end on the knit side. (Purl side is the right side.)

making up

With contrasting colors and yarn needle, add French knots to the stars. Place and sew the stars onto the hat as follows:

Side 1: Large and tiny star.

Side 2: Medium and little star.

Make two 2-inch tassels, holding dark blue and light blue strands together. Wrap 20 times. Attach to the points of the hat. If you like, secure the base of the tassel to the hat to stand straight up.

glossary

knitting terms

appliqué • A knitted piece added onto the knitted fabric by sewing it into place.

at the same time • Work more than one sequence or pattern simultaneously. For example, begin a decrease sequence and, at the same time, continue a stripe pattern previously being worked.

backward-loop cast-on • A simple way to cast on to begin a project or to add stitches in the middle of a row by creating a loop on the needle.

bind off • With two worked stitches on the right needle, pass the first stitch over the second stitch and off the needle. Used for finishing and taking the stitches off the needles at the end of a piece or for shaping as you are knitting. Binding off in the middle of a row can create a hole or buttonhole in the fabric.

cable needle • A small needle used to hold the stitches to the front or back of the work while creating the cable.

cast on • Creating a certain number of stitches on the needle, usually to begin a project. Can also be used for shaping or to create buttonholes or holes in the fabric. There are many techniques for casting on stitches.

decrease • Subtract from the number of stitches in a row or round.

embellishment • Decorative interest added after the knitted fabric is completed.

eyelet • A small hole created in the knitted fabric.

facing • The side of the knitted fabric facing you as you work.

garter stitch • Knit every row when knitting back and forth. Knit one round, purl one round when knitting in the round. Garter stitch creates a bumpy fabric that lies flat.

gauge • The number of stitches and rows per inch. Often, only the number of stitches per inch is listed and not the number of rows.

i-cord • A cording technique created by Elizabeth Zimmermann, using two double-pointed needles and sliding stitches to opposite ends of the needles to knit the cord.

increase • Add to the number of stitches in a row or round.

knit • Used as a verb to describe the act of knitting regardless of the stitch you are using. For example, "I love to knit." Also a stitch created with the yarn held to the back and the right needle inserted from left to right into the front of the stitch on the left needle.

knit in front and back of stitch • A common way to increase one stitch. Knit the stitch as usual, leaving the stitch on the left needle, then knit the same stitch again through the back loop to create the extra stitch. Drop the stitch from the left needle.

knitwise or as if to knit • Insert the needle into the next stitch as if to knit, from left to right.

long-tail cast-on • A common technique for casting on stitches. Start with a slip knot and leave a long end to use as stitches are added to the needle.

mattress stitch • A way to sew knitted fabric together to create a clean seam. Insert the yarn needle under two bars between the stitches going upward on one side and repeat on the other side to create the seam.

pick up and knit • Insert the needle into a finished edge and pull up loops to use as stitches to add an edging or to continue knitting from.

picot edge • A delicate decorative edging with textural interest.

purl • A stitch created with the yarn held in front and the right needle inserted from right to left into the front of the stitch on the left needle.

purl in front and back of stitch • A way to increase one stitch. Purl the next stitch as usual, leaving the stitch on the left needle, then insert the needle through the back loop from left to right and purl again to create the extra stitch. Then drop the stitch from the left needle.

purlwise or as if to purl • Insert the needle into the next stitch as if to purl, from right to left.

reverse stockinette stitch • Purl one row, knit one row when knitting back and forth. Purl every round when knitting in the round. The right side of the fabric is the purl side; this is the opposite of stockinette stitch.

rib stitch • Using a combination of knit and purl stitches in a series of rows to create a ribbed pattern. Ribbing is often used as an edging because it lies flat.

right side • The side of the knitted fabric that will be on the outside; the side that will show.

round • When working on circular or double-pointed needles with stitches joined together to create a circle, a round is one complete circle from the first stitch to the last.

seed stitch • Knit one stitch, purl one stitch across the row or round. Then do the opposite on the next row or round—purl the knit stitches and knit the purl stitches. This creates a textured fabric that is often used for edgings because it lies flat.

slip knot • Used as the first stitch on the needle when casting on stitches. Created by making a loop in the yarn and pulling another loop through it.

slip stitch, slip stitch, knit 2 slipped stitches together through the back loops • A way to make a right-slanting decrease. One at a time, slip the next two stitches knitwise to the right needle. Insert the left needle through the front loops of the two slipped stitches and knit these stitches together through the back loops.

slip stitch • Pass the stitch from the left needle to the right needle without making a new stitch. The directions will specify whether to slip as if to knit or knitwise, or slip as if to purl or purlwise.

stitch • A loop on the needle or in the knitted fabric.

stitch marker • A small ring that is slipped onto the needle to mark the beginning of a round when working in the round. Stitch markers can also be used as a guide to mark stitches in the middle of a row or round for stitch patterns. The marker is slipped from needle to needle as you work. Stitch markers can also be attached to the stitch loop to mark rows.

stockinette stitch • Knit one row, purl one row when knitting back and forth. Knit every round when knitting in the round. The edge of stockinette stitch fabric will naturally roll up. The right side of stockinette stitch is the knit side.

through back loop • Insert the needle into the back loop of the stitch.

turn work • Turn the work around in your hands to go the other direction. This can be done at any point in the row.

weaving in ends • To prevent unraveling, the tail end of the yarn is woven into the fabric using a yarn needle or crochet hook.

work even • Work without increasing or decreasing.

work to end • Work in the stitch pattern being used to the end of the row.

working yarn • Yarn attached to the ball.

wrong side • The side of the knitted fabric that will be on the inside of the piece; the side that won't show.

yarn over • Bringing the yarn over the right needle to create an added stitch. Yarn over is used when making eyelets, buttonholes, or decorative stitches.

crochet terms

chain stitch • The foundation row for beginning a crochet project. Start with a slip knot on the hook. Then yarn over and pull the loop through the stitch on the hook. Also used for decorative elements.

loop stitch • A stitch used to create loops in the fabric. Usually added as decoration after a project is completed; can be used as an edging.

single crochet • A basic crochet stitch. Created by pulling one loop through a stitch, yarning over, and pulling this loop through both of the loops on the hook.

slip knot • The first stitch on the hook. Created by making a loop in the yarn and pulling another loop through.

slip stitch • Often used to join a round. Created by pulling one loop through both a made stitch and the stitch already on the hook.

yarn over • Bring the yarn around the crochet hook.

embroidery terms

backstitch • A stitch used for outlining shapes or making small decorative stitches. The stitches are continuous.

french knot • A decorative technique used in numerous ways to create tiny bobbles on the fabric. When used close together, they can fill in space.

running stitch • A stitch used for sewing two pieces together and for outlining. The stitches have spaces in between.

satin stitch • A stitch used to fill in space by making parallel stitches close together.

straight stitch • A stitch used to form shapes such as circles, flowers, or leaves.

whipstitch • A decorative stitch used to sew two pieces together at the edges.

sources

Classic Elite Yarns
122 Western Ave.
Lowell, MA 01851
800-343-0308
www.classiceliteyarns.com

Colinette Yarns
Distributed by Unique Kolours
28 N. Bacton Rd.
Malvern, PA 19355
800-252-3934
www.uniquekolours.com

Debbie Bliss Yarns
Distributed by Knitting Fever
35 Debevoise Ave.
Roosevelt, NY 11575
800-645-3457
www.knittingfever.com

Fleurishes (ribbon)
2848 University Ave.
Madison, WI 53705
608-238-5555

GGH
Distributed by Muench Yarns
(GGH)
1323 Scott St.
Petaluma, CA 94954
800-733-9276
www.muenchyarns.com

Manos del Uruguay
Distributed by Design Source
P.O. Box 770
Medford, MA 02155
888-566-9970

Noro
Distributed by Knitting Fever
35 Debevoise Ave.
Roosevelt, NY 11575
800-645-3457
www.knittingfever.com

Rowan and RYC
Distributed by Westminster
Fibers
4 Townsend West, Unit 8
Nashua, NH 03063
603-886-5041
www.knitrowan.com
www.ryclassic.com

Tahki • Stacy Charles, Inc.
70-30 80th St.
Building 36
Ridgewood, NY 11385
800-338-9276
www.tahkistacycharles.com

knitting books and more

I am a knitting book fanatic. I collect, read, and reread any and all of the knitting books I can get my hands on. When I first began knitting in the 1980s, very few knitting books were available. Now I can't get over the shelves and shelves of knitting books at every bookstore. I vividly remember buying my first large hardcover knitting book when I was in graduate school. I don't think I have ever loved or read a book more than I did this one. I scoured this book instead of studying for my classes. I still get this absorbed when I find a new beautiful knitting book.

I have an extensive and ever-expanding knitting library that I keep close at hand in my knitting studio at home. I love to have these books at my house for inspiration, to look up any information I may need, and to admire their beauty. I recommend that every knitter have knitting and reference books at home; it will make your knitting life much easier and richer.

The authors and designers here have inspired me to no end, and I thank them. These are some of my favorites knitting books, Web sites, and magazines.

instructional

The Crocheter's Companion by Nancy Brown
How to Knit by Debbie Bliss
Kaffe Fassett's Pattern Library by Kaffe Fassett
Kids Embroidery by Kristin Nicholas
Kids Knitting by Melanie Falick
Knitted Embellishments by Nicky Epstein
The Knitter's Companion by Vicki Square
Knitting on the Edge by Nicky Epstein
Knitting Over the Edge by Nicky Epstein
Knitting Without Tears by Elizabeth Zimmermann
Knitting Workbook by Debbie Bliss
The Ultimate Knitter's Guide by Kate Buller

books with projects for everyone

Alterknits by Leigh Radford
Family Album by Kaffe Fassett and Zoë Hunt
Great Knitted Gifts by Andrea Shackleton and
    Gayle Shackleton
Hollywood Knits by Suss Cousins
Instant Expert: Knitting by Ros Badger
Knitting by Sarah Dallas
Knitting in America by Melanie Falick
Last-Minute Knitted Gifts by Joelle Hoverson
Loop-d-Loop by Teva Durham
Simple Chic by Jill Eaton
Stitch 'n Bitch by Debbie Stoller
Susan Duckworth's Knitting by Susan Duckworth
A Treasury of Rowan Knits edited by
    Stephen Sheard
Weekend Knitting by Melanie Falick

the internet and knitting

Visit Susan Anderson's Web site to purchase
knitting kits for this book and other baby goodies
at www.shopabcsoup.com.
Other helpful sites are:
www.jimmybeanswool.com
www.knitcast.com
www.knitrowan.com
www.knitty.com
www.learntoknit.com
www.patternworks.com
www.purlsoho.com
www.woolconnection.com
www.yarnco.com
www.yarnmarket.com

babies and children

The Baby Knits Book by Debbie Bliss
Baby Knits for Beginners by Debbie Bliss
Easy Knits by Debbie Bliss
50 Baby Bootees to Knit by Zoë Mellor
Handknits for Kids by Lucinda Guy
Head to Toe Knits by Zoë Mellor
Jaeger Handknits for Babies and Children by
    Martin Storey
Junior Knits by Debbie Bliss
Kids Crochet by Kelli Ronci
Kids' Knits for Heads, Hands & Toes
    by Debbie Bliss
Knitting for Baby by Melanie Falick and
    Kristin Nicholas
Knitting for Two by Erika Knight
Minnies by Jill Eaton
Miss Bea Collections by Louisa Harding
Pipsqueaks by Kim Hargreaves
Quick Baby Knits by Debbie Bliss
Rowan Babies by Kim Hargreaves
Rowan Junior by Kim Hargreaves
Simple Knits for Cherished Babies by
    Erika Knight
Simple Knits for Little Cherubs by Erika Knight
Special Knits by Debbie Bliss
Tadpoles & Tiddlers by Rowan Designers
Teen Knitting Club by Jennifer Wenger, Carol
    Abrams, and Maureen Lasher
Wee Knits and *Wee Knits, too* by Mags Kandis
    for Mission Falls

knitting magazines

Family Circle Easy Knitting
Interweave Knits
Knitter's Magazine
Knitting (printed in England)
Rowan Knitting Magazines (printed in England)
Simply Knitting (printed in England)
Vogue Knitting

acknowledgments

For me, knitting never ends, nor does my gratitude to all who helped create this book. First and foremost, thank you to Artisan Books for giving me this opportunity, which has been an extraordinary dream and hugely gratifying. Especially thanks to Ellice Goldstein for keeping up with my ongoing questions and concerns with a sense of humor and much knowledge as I have tried to figure out the art of book writing. Ellice, thanks for being my right hand through all of this. Thank you to Ann Bramson for seeing my potential and giving me this chance to shine. I felt challenged in the most positive way. Thank you to everyone at Artisan for your dedication in making this experience a smooth and joyful one.

Thank you to Betty Christiansen for copyediting. Your hard work in getting this book ready for release is greatly appreciated. I am indebted to your vast knowledge and expertise in all things knitting. Great appreciation to Jan Derevjanik for her book design talents.

Thank you to Liz Banfield for the delicious baby photography. Liz, you are such a talent. Grier's birth and this book will forever be entwined. I am honored. Much appreciation goes to all of the beautiful models and their parents for loaning their children to us. Cole, Audrey, Anne, Nicole, Sylvie, Derek, Macauley, Marilynn, Mary Margaret, Maria, Elizabeth, Luisa, Catherine, Alden, Zoe, Cody, Finley, Sargent, Charlotte, Julia, Elizabeth, Brooke, Max, Grier, William, and Andrew, you are all exquisite.

Personally, I want to shower my undying gratitude on my lovable family for letting me knit and write for hours at a time through thick and thin and even the summer. Brian, it's because of you that I am able to pursue my dreams. Thank you for the support, you truly are the best. You've made all of our wishes come true. Evan, Ben, Holly, and Mary Kate, thanks for giving me the best job in the world, being your mother. You are kind and patient people. All four of you inspire me every day. Mom, thanks for being my number-one fan and for all of the help and positive support you give on a daily basis. Dawn, Peter, and Scott Barrett, thanks for making me the luckiest sister in the world.

Thank you to Jim and Laura Mueller for spur-of-the-moment author photography and divine friendship.

Thank you to Kärren Murray, my friend and business partner, for letting me join you at Alphabet Soup. It was such creative fun, and it spurred me on to write this book. I appreciate all you've done.

Finally, thanks to all of the knitters at Alphabet Soup who made our shop the fun place that it was. I learned so much from you all.